ISBN 978-1-331-95877-2
PIBN 10259803

1 MONTH OF FREE READING

at

www.ForgottenBooks.com

By purchasing this book you are eligible for one month membership to ForgottenBooks.com, giving you unlimited access to our entire collection of over 1,000,000 titles via our web site and mobile apps.

To claim your free month visit:

www.forgottenbooks.com/free259803

English
Français
Deutsche
Italiano
Español
Português

www.forgottenbooks.com

Mythology Photography **Fiction**
Fishing Christianity **Art** Cooking
Essays Buddhism Freemasonry
Medicine **Biology** Music **Ancient
Egypt** Evolution Carpentry Physics
Dance Geology **Mathematics** Fitness
Shakespeare **Folklore** Yoga Marketing
Confidence Immortality Biographies
Poetry **Psychology** Witchcraft
Electronics Chemistry History **Law**
Accounting **Philosophy** Anthropology
Alchemy Drama Quantum Mechanics
Atheism Sexual Health **Ancient History**
Entrepreneurship Languages Sport
Paleontology Needlework Islam
Metaphysics Investment Archaeology
Parenting Statistics Criminology
Motivational

THE

WONDERS OF POMPEII.

BY

MARC MONNIER.

TRANSLATED FROM THE ORIGINAL FRENCH.

NEW YORK:

CHARLES SCRIBNER & CO.,

654 BROADWAY.

1871.

Illustrated Library of Wonders.

PUBLISHED BY

Messrs. Charles Scribner & Co.,

654 BROADWAY, NEW YORK.

Each one volume 12mo. ;   Price per volume, $1.50

The above works sent to any address, post-paid, upon receipt of the price by the publishers.

LIST OF ILLUSTRATIONS.

.

CONTENTS.

I.

THE EXHUMED CITY.

II.

THE FORUM.

VIII.

THE THEATRES.

IX.

THE ERUPTION.

DIALOGUE.

A TRAVELLER (*entering*). — Have you any work on Pompeii?

THE SALESMAN. — Yes; we have several. Here, for instance, is Bulwer's "Last Days of Pompeii."

TRAVELLER. — Too thoroughly romantic. .

SALESMAN. — Well, here are the folios of Mazois.

TRAVELLER. — Too heavy.

SALESMAN. — Here's Dumas's "Corricolo."

TRAVELLER. — Too light.

SALESMAN. — How would Nicolini's magnificent work suit you?

TRAVELLER. — Oh! that's too dear.

SALESMAN. — Here's Commander Aloë's "Guide."

TRAVELLER. — That's too dry.

SALESMAN.—Neither dry, nor romantic, nor light, nor heavy! What, then, would you have, sir?

TRAVELLER.— A small, portable work; accurate, conscientious, and within everybody's reach.

SALESMAN. — Ah, sir, we have nothing of that kind; besides, it is impossible to get up such a work.

THE AUTHOR (*aside*).—Who knows?

THE

WONDERS OF POMPEII.

I.

THE EXHUMED CITY.

THE ANTIQUE LANDSCAPE — THE HISTORY OF POMPEII BEFORE AND AFTER ITS DESTRUCTION. — HOW IT WAS BURIED AND EXHUMED. — WINKELMANN AS A PROPHET. — THE EXCAVATIONS IN THE REIGN OF CHARLES III., OF MURAT, AND OF FERDINAND. — THE EXCAVATIONS AS THEY NOW ARE. — SIGNOR FIORELLI. — APPEARANCE OF THE RUINS. — WHAT IS AND WHAT IS NOT FOUND THERE.

A RAILROAD runs from Naples to Pompeii. Are you alone? The trip occupies one hour, and you have just time enough to read what follows, pausing once in a while to glance at Vesuvius and the sea; the clear, bright waters hemmed in by the gentle curve of the promontories; a bluish coast that approaches and becomes green; a green coast that withdraws into the distance and becomes blue; Castellamare looming up, and Naples receding. All these lines and colors existed

2

too at the time when Pompeii was destroyed: the island of Prochyta, the cities of Baiæ, of Bauli, of Neapolis, and of Surrentum bore the names that they retain. Portici was called Herculaneum; Torre dell' Annunziata was called Oplontes; Castellamare, Stabiæ; Misenum and Minerva designated the two extremities of the gulf. However, Vesuvius was not what it has become; fertile and wooded almost to the summit, covered with orchards and vines, it must have resembled the picturesque heights of Monte San Angelo, toward which we are rolling. The summit alone, honeycombed with caverns and covered with black stones, betrayed to the learned a volcano "long extinct." It was to blaze out again, however, in a terrible eruption; and, since then, it has constantly flamed and smoked, menacing the ruins it has made and the new cities that brave it, calmly reposing at its feet.

What do you expect to find at Pompeii? At a distance, its antiquity seems enormous, and the word "ruins" awakens colossal conceptions in the excited fancy of the traveller. But, be not self-deceived; that is the first rule in knocking about over the world. Pompeii was a small city of only thirty thousand souls;

something like what Geneva was thirty years ago.
Like Geneva, too, it was marvellously situated—in the
depth of a picturesque valley between mountains shut
ting in the horizon on one side, at a few steps from
the sea and from a streamlet, once a river, which
plunges into it—and by its charming site attracted
personages of distinction, although it was peopled
chiefly with merchants and others in easy circum-
stances; shrewd, prudent folk, and probably honest
and clever enough, as well. The etymologists, after
having exhausted, in their lexicons, all the words that
chime in sound with Pompeii, have, at length, agreed
in deriving the name from a Greek verb which signifies *to send, to transport*, and hence they conclude
that many of the Pompeians were engaged in exporta-
tion, or perhaps, were emigrants sent from a distance
to form a colony. Yet these opinions are but conjec-
tures, and it is useless to dwell on them.

All that can be positively stated is that the city was
the entrepôt of the trade of Nola, Nocera, and Atella.
Its port was large enough to receive a naval armament,
for it sheltered the fleet of P. Cornelius. This port,
mentioned by certain authors, has led many to believe

that the sea washed the walls of Pompeii, and some
guides have even thought they could discover the rings
that once held the cables of the galleys. Unfortunately for this idea, at the place which the imagination
of some of our contemporaries covered with salt water,
there were one day discovered the vestiges of old
structures, and it is now conceded that Pompeii, like
many other seaside places, had its harbor at a distance.

Our little city made no great noise in history. Taci-
tus and Seneca speak of it as celebrated, but the
Italians of all periods have been fond of superlatives.
You will find some very old buildings in it, proclaiming an ancient origin, and Oscan inscriptions recalling
the antique language of the country. When the Samnites invaded the whole of Campania, as though to
deliver it over more easily to Rome, they probably
occupied Pompeii, which figured in the second Samnite war, B. C. 310, and which, revolting along with
the entire valley of the Sarno from Nocera to Stabiæ,
repulsed an incursion of the Romans and drove them
back to their vessels. The third Samnite war was, as
is well known, a bloody vengeance for this, and Pompeii became Roman. Although the yoke of the con-

querors was not very heavy — the *municipii* retaining their Senate, their magistrates, their *comitiæ* or councils, and paying a tribute of men only in case of war — the Samnite populations, clinging frantically to the idea of a separate and independent existence, rose twice again in revolt; once just after the battle of Cannæ, when they threw themselves into the arms of Hannibal, and then against Sylla, one hundred and twenty-four years later — facts that prove the tenacity of their resistance. On both occasions Pompeii was retaken, and the second time partly dismantled and occupied by a detachment of soldiers, who did not long remain there. And thus we have the whole history of this little city. The Romans were fond of living there, and Cicero had a residence in the place, to which he frequently refers in his letters. Augustus sent thither a colony which founded the suburb of Augustus Felix, administered by a mayor. The Emperor Claudius also had a villa at Pompeii, and there lost one of his children, who perished by a singular mishap. The imperial lad was amusing himself, as the Neapolitan boys do to this day, by throwing pears up into the air and catching them in his mouth as they fell. One of the fruits

2*

choked him by descending too far into his throat.
But the Neapolitan youngsters perform the feat with
figs, which render it infinitely less dangerous.

We are, then, going to visit a small city subordinate
to Rome, much less than Marseilles is to Paris, and a
little more so than Geneva is to Berne. Pompeii had
almost nothing to do with the Senate or the Emperor.
The old tongue — the Oscan — had ceased to be official, and the authorities issued their orders in Latin.
The residents of the place were Roman citizens, Rome
being recognized as the capital and fatherland. The
local legislation was made secondary to Roman legisla-
lation. But, excepting these reservations, Pompeii
formed a little world, apart, independent, and complete
in itself. She had a miniature Senate, composed of
decurions; an aristocracy in epitome, represented by
the *Augustales*, answering to knights; and then came
her *plebs* or common people. She chose her own
pontiffs, convoked the comitiæ, promulged municipal
laws, regulated military levies, collected taxes; in fine
selected her own immediate rulers — her consuls (the
duumvirs dispensing justice), her ediles, her quæstors,
etc. Hence, it is not a provincial city that we are to

survey, but a petty State which had preserved its autonomy within the unity of the Empire, and was, as has been cleverly said, a miniature of Rome.

Another circumstance imparts a peculiar interest to Pompeii. That city, which seemed to have no good luck, had been violently shaken by earthquake in the year B. C. 63. Several temples had toppled down along with the colonnade of the Forum, the great Basilica, and the theatres, without counting the tombs and houses. Nearly every family fled from the place, taking with them their furniture and their statuary; and the Senate hesitated a long time before they allowed the city to be rebuilt and the deserted district to be re-peopled. The Pompeians at last returned; but the decurions wished to make the restoration of the place a complete rejuvenation. The columns of the Forum speedily reappeared, but with capitals in the fashion of the day; the Corinthian-Roman order, adopted almost everywhere, changed the style of the monuments; the old shafts covered with stucco were patched up for the new topwork they were to receive, and the Oscan inscriptions disappeared. From all this there sprang great blunders in an artistic point of

view, but a uniformity and consistency that please
those who are fond of monuments and cities of one
continuous derivation.   Taste loses, but harmony gains
thereby, and you pass in review a collective totality of
edifices that bear their age upon their fronts, and give
a very exact and vivid idea of what a *municeps* a
Roman colony must have been in the time of Vespasian.

They went to work, then, to rebuild the city, and
the undertaking was pushed on quite vigorously,
thanks to the contributions of the Pompeians, especially of the functionaries.   The temples of Jupiter
and of Venus — we adopt the consecrated names —
and those of Isis and of Fortune, were already up; the
theatres were rising again; the handsome columns of
the Forum were ranging themselves under their porticoes; the residences were gay with brilliant paintings;
work and pleasure had both resumed their activity;
life hurried to and fro through the streets, and crowds
thronged the amphitheatre, when, all at once, burst
forth the terrible eruption of 79.   I will describe it
further on; but here simply recall the fact that it
buried Pompeii under a deluge of stones and ashes.

This re-awakening of the volcano destroyed three cities, without counting the villages, and depopulated the country in the twinkling of an eye.

After the catastrophe, however, the inhabitants returned, and made the first excavations in order to recover their valuables; and robbers, too—we shall surprise them in the very act—crept into the subterranean city. It is a fact that the Emperor Titus for a moment entertained the idea of clearing and restoring it, and with that view sent two Senators to the spot, intrusted with the mission of making the first study of the ground; but it would appear that the magnitude of the work appalled those dignitaries, and that the restoration in question never got beyond the condition of a mere project. Rome soon had more serious cares to occupy her than the fate of a petty city that ere long disappeared beneath vineyards, orchards, and gardens, and under a thick growth of woodland—remark this latter circumstance—until, at length, centuries accumulated, and with them the forgetfulness that buries all things. Pompeii was then, so to speak, lost, and the few learned men who knew it by name could not point out its site. When, at the close of the

sixteenth century, the architect Fontana was con-
structing a subterranean canal to convey the waters of
the Sarno to Torre dell' Annunziata, the conduit
passed through Pompeii, from one end to the other,
piercing the walls, following the old streets, and coming upon sub structures and inscriptions; but no one
bethought him that they had discovered the place of
the buried city.   However, the amphitheatre, which,
roofed in by a layer of the soil, formed a regular ex-
cavation, indicated an ancient edifice, and the neighboring peasantry, with better information than the
learned, designated by the half-Latin name of *Civita*,
which dim tradition had handed down, the soil and
debris that had accumulated above Pompeii.

It was only in 1748, under the reign of Charles III,
when the discovery of Herculaneum had attracted the
attention of the world to the antiquities thus buried,
that, some vine-dressers having struck upon some old
walls with their picks and spades, and in so doing
unearthed statues, a colonel of engineers named Don
Rocco Alcubierra asked permission of the king to
make excavations in the vicinity.   The king consented
and placed a dozen of galley-slaves at the colonel's

disposition. Thus it was that by a lucky chance a military engineer discovered the city that we are about to visit. Still, eight years more had to roll away before any one suspected that it was Pompeii which they were thus exhuming. Learned folks thought they were dealing with Stabiæ.

Shall I relate the history of these underground researches, "badly conducted, frequently abandoned, and resumed in obedience to the same capriciousness that had led to their suspension," as they were? Such are the words of the opinion Barthelemy expressed when writing, in 1755, to the Count de Caylus. Winkelmann, who was present at these excavations a few years later, sharply criticised the tardiness of the galley-slaves to whom the work had been confided. "At this rate," he wrote, "our descendants of the fourth generation will still have digging to do among these ruins." The illustrious German hardly suspected that he was making so accurate a prediction as it has turned out to be. The descendants of the fourth generation are our contemporaries, and the third part of Pompeii is not yet unearthed.

The Emperor Joseph II. visited the excavations on

the 6th of April, 1796, and complained bitterly to
King Ferdinand IV. of the slight degree of zeal and
the small amount of money employed. The king
promised to do better, but did not keep his word. He
had neither. intelligence nor activity in prosecuting
this immense task, excepting while the French occu-
pation lasted. At that time, however, the government
carried out the idea of Francesco La Vega, a man of
sense and capacity, and purchased all the ground that
covered Pompeii. Queen Caroline, the sister of Bona-
parte and wife of Murat, took a fancy to these
excavations and pushed them vigorously, often going
all the way from Naples through six leagues of dust to
visit them. In 1813 there were exactly four hundred
and seventy-six laborers employed at Pompeii. The
Bourbons returned and commenced by re-selling the
ground that had been purchased under Murat; then,
little by little, the work continued, at first with some
activity, then fell off and slackened more and more
until, from being neglected, they were altogether abandoned, and were resumed only once in a while in the
presence of crowned heads. On these occasions they
were got up like New Year's surprise games: every-

thing that happened to be at hand was scattered about on layers of ashes and of pumice-stone and carefully covered over. Then, upon the arrival of such-and-such a majesty, or this or that highness, the magic wand of the superintendent or inspector of the works caused all these treasures to spring out of the ground. I could name, one after the other, the august personages who were deceived in this manner, beginning with the Kings of the Two Sicilies and of Jerusalem.

But that is not all. Not only was nothing more discovered at Pompeii, but even the monuments that had been found were not preserved. King Ferdinand soon discovered that the 25,000 francs applied to the excavations were badly employed; he reduced the sum to 10,000, and that amount was worn down on the way by passing through so many hands. Pompeii fell back, gradually presenting nothing but ruins upon ruins.

Happily, the Italian Government established by the revolution of 1860, came into power to set all these acts of negligence and roguery to rights. Signor Fiorelli, who is all intelligence and activity, not to mention his erudition, which numerous writings prove, was appointed inspector of the excavations.

3

Under his administration, the works which had been vigorously resumed were pushed on by as many as seven hundred laborers at a time, and they dug out in the lapse of three years more treasures than had been brought to light in the thirty that preceded them. Everything has been reformed, nay, *moralized*, as it were, in the dead city; the visitor pays two francs at the gate and no longer has to contend with the horde of guides, doorkeepers, rapscallions, and beggars who formerly plundered him. A small museum, recently established, furnishes the active inquirer the opportunity of examining upon the spot the curiosities that have already been discovered; a library containing the fine works of Mazois, of Raoul Rochette, of Gell, of Zahn, of Overbeck, of Breton, etc., on Pompeii, enables the student to consult them in Pompeii itself; workshops lately opened are continually busy in restoring cracked walls, marbles, and bronzes, and one may there surprise the artist Bramante, the most ingenious hand at repairing antiquities in the world, as likewise my friend, Padiglione, who, with admirable patience and minute fidelity, is cutting a small model in cork of the ruins that have been cleared, which is scrupulously exact. In fine—and this is the main point—the excavations are no longer carried on occasionally only, and in the presence of a few privileged persons, but before the first comer and every day, unless funds have run short.

"I have frequently been present," wrote a half-Pompeian, a year or two ago, in the *Revue des Deux Mondes*—"I have frequently been present for hours together, seated on a sand-bank which itself, perhaps, concealed wonders, and witnessed this rude yet interesting toil, from which I could not withdraw my gaze. I therefore have it in my power to write understandingly. I do not relate what I read, but what I saw. Three systems, to my knowledge, have been employed in these excavations. The first, inaugurated under Charles III., was the simplest. It consisted in hollowing out the soil, in extricating the precious objects found, and then in re-filling the orifice—an excellent method of forming a museum by destroying Pompeii. This method was abandoned so soon as it was discovered that a whole city was involved. The second system, which was gradually brought to perfection in the last century, was earnestly pursued under Murat. The work was started in many places at once, and the laborers, advancing one after the other, penetrating and cut-,ing the hill, followed the line of the streets, which they cleared little by little before them. In following the streets on the ground-level, the declivity of ashes and pumice-stone which obstructed them was attacked below, and thence resulted many regrettable accidents. The whole upper part of the houses, commencing with the roofs, fell in among the rubbish, along with a thousand fragile articles, which were broken and lost without there being any means of determining the point from which ʹhey had been hurled down. In order to obviate ʹhis inconvenience, Signor Fiorelli has started a ,hird system. He does not follow the streets by the ground-level, but he marks them out over the hillocks, and thus traces among the trees and cultivated grounds wide squares indicating the subterranean islets. No one is ignorant of the fact ;hat these islets—*isole, insulæ* in the modern as well as in the ancient language of Italy—indicate blocks

of buildings. The islet traced, Signor Fiorelli re-
purchases the land which had been sold by King
Ferdinand I. and gives up the trees found upon
it.*

"The ground, then, being bought and the vegetation removed, work begins. The earth at the summit of the hill is taken off and carried away on
a railroad, which descends from the middle of Pompeii by a slope that saves all expense of machinery and fuel, to a considerable distance beyond
the amphitheatre and the city. In this way, the
most serious question of all, to wit, that of clearing
away the dirt, is solved. Formerly, the ruins were
covered in with it, and subsequently it was heaped
up in a huge hillock, but now it helps to construct
the very railroad that carries it away, and will, one
day, tip it into the sea.

"Nothing can present a livelier scene than the ex-
cavation of these ruins. Men diligently dig away at
the earth, and bevies of young girls run to and fro
without cessation, with baskets in their hands. These

---

* The money accruing from this sale is applied to the Pompeian
library mentioned elsewhere.

3*

are sprightly peasant damsels collected from the adjacent villages most of them accustomed to working in
factories that have closed or curtailed operations owing
to the invasion of English tissues and the rise of
cotton. No one would have dreamed that free trade
and the war in America would have supplied female
hands to work at the ruins of Pompeii. But all things
are linked together now in this great world of ours,
vast as it is. These girls then run backward and
forward, filling their baskets with soil, ashes, and
lapillo, hoisting them on their heads, by the help
of the men, with a single quick, sharp motion, and
thereupon setting off again, in groups that incessantly
replace each other, toward the railway, passing and re-
passing their returning companions. Very picturesque
in their ragged gowns of brilliant colors, they walk
swiftly with lengthy strides, their long skirts defining
the movements of their naked limbs and fluttering in
the wind behind them, while their arms, with gestures like those of classic urn-bearers, sustain the heavy
load that rests upon their heads without making them
even stoop. All this is not out of keeping with the
monuments that gradually appear above the surface as

The Rubbish Trucks Going up Empty.

the rubbish is removed. Did not the sight of foreign visitors here and there disturb the harmony of the scene, one might readily ask himself, in the midst of this Virgilian landscape, amid these festooning vines, in full view of the smoking Vesuvius, and beneath that antique sky, whether all those young girls who come and go are not the slaves of Pansa, the aedile, or of the duumvir Holconius."

We have just glanced over the history of Pompeii before and after its destruction. Let us now enter the city. But a word of caution before we start. Do not expect to find houses or monuments still erect and roofed in like the Pantheon at Rome and the square building at Nismes, or you will be sadly disappointed. Rather picture to yourself a small city of low buildings and narrow streets that had been completely burned down in a single night. You have come to look at it on the day after the conflagration. The upper stories have disappeared, and the ceilings have fallen in. Everything that was of wood, planks, and beams, is in ashes; all is uncovered, and no roofs are to be seen. In these structures, which in other days were either private dwellings or public edifices, you now can everywhere walk under the open sky. Were a shower to come on, you would not know where to seek shelter. It is as though you were in a city in progress of building, with only the first stories as yet completed, but without the flooring for the second. Here is a house: nothing remains of it but the lower walls, with nothing resting on them. At a distance you would suppose it to be a collection of screens set up for parlor theatricals. Here is a public square: you will now see in it only bottom platforms, supports that hold up nothing, shafts of columns without galleries, pedestals without statues, mute blocks of stone, space and emptiness. I will lead you into more than one temple. You will see there only an eminence of masonry, side and end walls, but no front, no portico. Where is art? Where is the presiding deity of the place? The ruins of your stable would not be more naked a thousand years hence. Stones on all sides, tufa, bricks, lava, here and there some slabs of marble and travertine, then traces of destruction—paintings defaced, pavements disjointed and full of gaps and cracks—and then marks of spoliation, for all the precious objects found were carried off to the museum

Clearing out a Narrow Street in Pompeii.

at Naples, and I can show you now nothing but the places where once stood the Faun, the statue of Narcissus, the mosaic of Arbelles and the famous blue vase. Such is the Pompeii that awaits the traveller who comes thither expecting to find another Paris, or, at least, ruins arranged in the Parisian style, like the tower of St. Jacques, for instance.

You will say, perhaps, good reader, that I disenchant you; on the contrary, I prevent your disenchantment. Do not prepare the way for your own disappointment by unreasonable expectations or by ill-founded notions; this is all that I ask of your judgment. Do not come hither to look for the relics of Roman grandeur. Other impressions await you at Pompeii. What you are about to see is an entire city, or at all events the third of an ancient city, remote, detached from every modern town, and forming in itself something isolated and complete which you will find nowhere else. Here is no Capitol rebuilt; no Pantheon consecrated now to the God of Christianity; no Acropolis surmounting a Danish or Bavarian city; no Maison Carrée (as at Nismes) transformed to a gallery of paintings and forming one of the adornments of a

modern Boulevard. At Pompeii everything is antique
and eighteen centuries old; first the sky, then the
landscape, the seashore, and then the work of man,
devastated undoubtedly, but not transformed, by time.
The streets are not repaired; the high sidewalks that
border them have not been lowered for the pedestrians
of our time, and we promenade upon the same stones
that were formerly trodden by the feet of Sericus
the merchant and Epaphras the slave. As we enter
these narrow streets we quit, perforce, the year in
which we are living and the quarter that we inhabit.
Behold us in a moment transported to another age
and into another world. Antiquity invades and
absorbs us and, were it but for an hour, we are
Romans. That, however, is not all. I have already
repeatedly said that Vesuvius did not destroy Pompeii
—it has preserved it.

The structures that have been exhumed crumble
away in the air in a few months — more than they had
done beneath the ashes in eighteen centuries. When
first disinterred the painted walls reappear fresh and
glowing as though their coloring were but of yester-
day. Each wall thus becomes, as it were, a page of

illustrated archeology, unveiling to us some point hitherto unknown of the manners, customs, private habits, creeds and traditions; or, to sum all up in a word, of the life of the ancients.

The furniture one finds, the objects of art or the household utensils, reveal to us the mansion; there is not a single panel which, when closely examined, does not tell us something. Such and such a pillar has retained the inscription scratched upon it with the point of his knife by a Pompeian who had nothing else to do; such a piece of wall on the street set apart for posters, presents in huge letters the announcement of a public spectacle, or proclaims the candidature of some citizen for a contested office of the state.

I say nothing of the skeletons, whose attitudes relate, in a most striking manner, the horrors of the catastrophe and the frantic struggles of the last moment. In fine, for any one who has the faculty of observation, every step is a surprise, a discovery, a confession won concerning the public and private life of the ancients. Although at first sight mute, these blocks of stone, when interrogated, soon speak and confide their secrets to science or to the imagination that catches a meaning with half a word; they tell, little by little, all that they know, and all the strange, mysterious things that took place on these same pavements, under this same sky, in those miraculous times, the most interesting in history, viz.: the eighth century of Rome and the first of the Christian era.

II.

THE FORUM.

As you alight at the station, in the first place breakfast at the *popina* of Diomed. It is a tavern of our own day, which has assumed an antique title to please travellers. You may there drink Falernian wine manufactured by Scala, the Neapolitan chemist, and, should you ask for some *jentaculum* in the Roman style — *aliquid scitamentorum, glandionidum suillam taridum, pernonidem, sinciput aut omenta porcina, aut aliquid ad eum modum* — they will serve you a beefsteak and potatoes. Your strength refreshed, you will scale the sloping hillock of ashes and rubbish that conceals the ruins from your view; you will pay your two francs at the office and you will pass the gate-keeper's turn-

4

stile, astonished, as it is, to find itself in such a place. These formalities once concluded you have nothing more that is modern to go through unless it be the companionship of a guide in military uniform who escorts you, in reality to *watch* you (especially if you belong to the country of Lord Elgin), but not to mulct you in the least. Placards in all the known languages forbid you to offer him so much as an *obolus*. You make your *entrée*, in a word, into the antique life, and you are as free as a Pompeian.

The first thing one sees is an arcade and such a niche as might serve for an image of the Madonna; but be reassured, for the niche contains a Minerva. It is no longer the superstition of our own time that strikes our gaze. Under the arcade open extensive store-houses that probably served as a place of deposit for merchandise. You then enter an ascending paved street, pass by the temple of Venus and the Basilica, and arrive at the Forum. There, one should pause.

At first glance, the observer distinguishes nothing but a long square space closed at the further extremity by a regular-shaped mound rising between two arcades; lateral alleys extend lengthwise on the right and the left

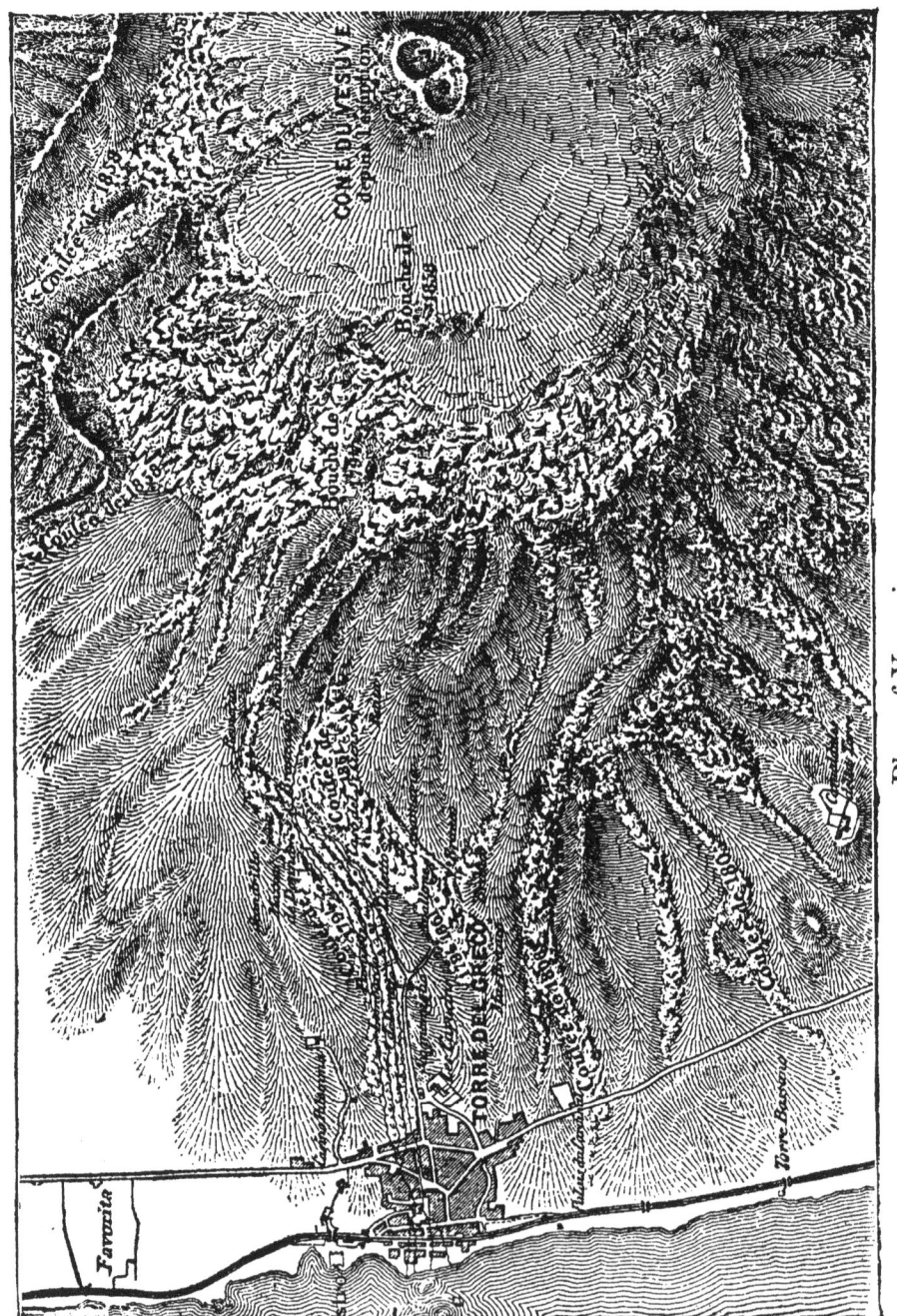

Plan of Vesuvius.

between shafts of columns and dilapidated architectural work. Here and there some compound masses of stone-work indicate altars or the pedestals of statues no longer seen. Vesuvius, still threatening, smokes away at the extremity of the picture.

Look more closely and you will perceive that the fluted columns are of Caserta stone, of tufa, or of brick, coated with stucco and raised two steps above the level of the square. Under the lower step runs the kennel. These columns sustained a gallery upon which one mounted by narrow and abrupt steps that time has spared. This upper gallery must have been covered. The women walked in it. A second story of columns, most likely interrupted in front of the monuments, rested upon the other one. Mazois has reconstructed this colonnade in two superior orders—Doric below and Ionic above — with exquisite elegance. The pavement of the square, on which you may still walk, was of travertine. Thus we see the Forum rising again, as it were, in our presence.

Let us glance at the ruins that surround it. That mound at the other end was the foundation of a temple, the diminutive size of which strikes the new-

comer at first sight. Every one is not aware that the
temple, far from being a place of assemblage for de-
vout multitudes, was, with the ancients, in reality, but
a larger niche inclosing the statue of the deity to be
worshipped. The consecrated building received only a
small number of the elect after they had been befit-
tingly purified, and the crowd remained outside. It
was not the palace, but the mere cell of the god. This
cell (*cella*) was, at first, the whole temple, and was just
large enough to hold the statue and the altar. By
degrees it came to be ornamented with a front portico,
then with a rear portico, and then with side colonnades, thus attaining by embellishment after embellishment the rich elegance of the Madeleine at Paris.
But the proportions of our cathedrals were never
adopted by the ancients. Thus, Christianity rarely
appropriates the Greek or Roman temples for its
worship. It has preferred the vast basilicas, the royal
name of which assumes a religious meaning.

The Romans built their temples in this wise: The
augur—that is to say, the priest who read the future
in the flight of birds—traced in the sky with his short
staff a spacious square, which he then marked on the

soil. Stakes were at once fixed along the four lines, and draperies were hung between the stakes. In the midst of this space, the area or inclosure of the temple, the augur marked out a cross—the augural cross, indicating the four cardinal points; the transverse lines fixed the limits of the *cella;* the point where the two branches met was the place for the door, and the first stone was deposited on the threshold. Numerous lighted lamps illuminated these ceremonies, after which the chief priest, the *pontifex maximus,* consecrated the area, and from that moment it became settled and immovable. If it crumbled, it must be rebuilt on the same spot, and the least change made, even should it be to enlarge it, would be regarded as a profanation. Thus had the dwelling of the god that rises before us at the extremity of the Forum been consecrated.

Like most of the Roman temples, this edifice is elevated on a foundation (the *podium*), and turned toward the north. One ascends to it by a flight of steps that cuts in the centre a platform where, perhaps, the altar stood. Upon the *podium* there remain some vestiges of the twelve columns that

formed the front portico or *pronaos*. Twelve columns, did I say?—three on each side, six in front;
always an even number at the facades, so that a
central column may not mask the doorway and that
the temple may be freely entered by the intercol-
umnar middle space.

To the right and the left of the steps were pedestals that formerly sustained statues probably colossal. Behind the *pronaos* could be recognized the
place where the *cella* used to be. Nothing remains
of it now but the mosaic pavement and the walls.
Traces of columns enable us to reconstruct this sanctuary richly. We can there raise—and it has been
done on paper—two colonnades—the first one of the
Ionic order, supporting a gallery; the second of the
Corinthian order, sustaining the light wooden platform of painted wood which no longer exists. The
walls, covered with stucco, still retain pretty decorative paintings. Three small subterranean chambers,
of very solid construction, perhaps contained the
treasury and archives of the State, or something else
entirely different—why not those of the temple?

THE FORUM.

In those times the Church was rich; the Saviour had not ordained poverty as its portion.

What deity's house is it that we are visiting now? Jupiter's, says common opinion, upon the strength of a colossal statue of which fragments have been found that might well have fitted the King of the Gods. Others think it the temple of Venus, the *Venus Physica* (the beautiful in nature, say æsthetic philosophers) being the patroness of Pompeii. We shall frequently, hereafter, meet with the name of this goddess. Several detached limbs in stone and in bronze, which are not broken at the extremity as though they belonged to a statue, but are polished on all sides and cut in such a manner as to admit of being suspended, were found among the ruins; they were votive offerings. Italy, in becoming Catholic, has retained these Pagan customs. Besides her supreme God, she worships a host of demi-gods, to whom she dedicates her towns and consecrates her temples, where garlands of ex-voto offerings testify to the intercession of the priests and the gratitude of the true believers.

On the two sides of the temple of Jupiter—such

is the generally-accepted name—rise arcades, as I have already remarked. The one on the left is a vaulted entrance, which, being too low and standing too far forward, does not correspond with the other and deranges, one cannot exactly make out why, the symmetry of this part of the Forum. The other arcade is evidently a triumphal portal. Nothing remains of it now but the body of the work in brick, some niches and traces of pilasters; but it is easy to replace the marbles and the statues which must have adorned this monument in rather poor taste. Such was the extremity of the Forum.

Four considerable edifices follow each other on the eastern side of this public square. These are, going from south to north, the palace of Eumachia, the temple of Mercury, the Senate Chamber, and the Pantheon.

What is the Eumachia palace? An inscription found at that place reads: "Eumachia, in her name and in the name of her son, has erected to Concord and to august Piety, a Chalcidicum, a crypt and porticoes."

What is a Chalcidicum? Long and grave have

been the discussions on this subject among the savans. They have agreed, however, on one point, that it should be a species of structure invented at Chalcis, a city of Eubea.

However that may be, this much-despoiled palace presents a vast open gallery, which was, certainly, the portico mentioned above. Around the portico ran a closed gallery along three sides, and that must have been the crypt. Upon the fourth side — that is to say, before the entry that fronts the Forum — stood forth a sort of porch, a large exterior vestibule : that was probably the Chalcidicum.

The edifice is curious. Behind the vestibule are two walls, not parallel, one of which follows the alignment of the Forum, and the other that of the interior portico. The space between this double wall is utilized and some shops hide themselves in its recesses. Thus the irregularity of the plan is not merely corrected—it is turned to useful account. The ancients were shrewd fellows. This portico rested on fifty-eight columns, surrounding a court-yard. In the court-yard, a large movable stone, in good preservation, with the ~ing that served to lift

it, covered a cistern. At the extremity of the por
tico, in a hemicycle, stood a headless statue — perhaps
the Piety or Concord to which the entire edifice was
dedicated. Behind the hemicycle a sort of square
niche buried itself in the wall between two doors,
one of which, painted on the wall for the sake of
symmetry, is a useful and curious document. It is
separated into three long and narrow panels and
is provided with a ring that should have served to
move it. Doors are nowhere to be seen now in
Pompeii, because they were of wood, and conse-
quently were consumed by the fire; hence, this
painted representation has filled the savants with
delight; they now know that the ancients shut
themselves in at home by processes exactly like our
own.

Between the two doors, in the square niche, the
statue of Eumachia, or, at least, a moulded model
of that statue, is still erect upon its pedestal. It
is of a female of tall stature, who looks sad and ill.
An inscription informs us that the statue was erected
in her honor by the fullers. These artisans formed
quite a respectable corporation at Pompeii, and we

shall presently visit the manufactory where they worked. Everything is now explained : the edifice of Eumachia must have been the Palace of Industry of that city and period. This is the Pompeian Merchants' Exchange, where transactions took place in the portico, and in winter, in the crypt. The tribunal of commerce sat in the hemicycle, at the foot of the statue of Concord, raised there to appease quarrels between the merchants. In the court-yard, the huge blocks of stone still standing were the tables on which their goods were spread. The cistern and the large vats yielded the conveniences to wash them. In fine, the Chalcidicum was the smaller Exchange, and the niches still seen there must have been the stands of the auctioneers. But what was there in common between this market, this fullers' counter, and the melancholy priestess?

Religion at that period entered into everything, even into trade and industry. A secret door put the edifice of Eumachia in communication with the adjacent temple. That temple, which was dedicated to Mercury — why to Mercury ? — or to Quirinus — why *not* to Mercury ?—at this day forms a small museum of

precious relics. The entrance to it is closed with a
grating through which a sufficient view may be had of
the bas-relief on the altar, representing a sacrifice. A
personage whose head is half-veiled presides at the
ceremony ; behind that person a child carries the
consecrated water in a vase, and the *victimarius,*
bearing an axe, leads the bull that is to be offered up.
Behind the sacrificial party are some flute-players.
On the two sides of the altar other bas-reliefs represent the instruments that were used at the sacrifices ;
the *lituus,* or curved staff of the augur; the *acerra,*
or perfuming censer; the *mantile,* or consecrated cloth
that — let us simply say, the napkin, — and, finally, the
vases peculiar to these ceremonies, the *patere,* the
simpulum, and the *prefericulum.*

That altar is the only curiosity in the temple. The
remainder is not worth the trouble of being studied
or reconstructed. The mural paintings form an
adornment of questionable taste. A rear door puts
the temple in communication with the *Senaculum,* or
Senate-house, as the neighboring structure was called ;
but the Pompeian Senators being no more than decurions, it is an ambitious title. A vestibule that

comes forward as far as the colonnade of the Forum; then a spacious saloon or hall; an arch at the end, with a broad foundation where the seats of the decemviri possibly stood; then, walls built of rough stones arranged in net-work (*opus reticulatum*), some niches without statues — such is all that remains. But with a ceiling of wood painted in bright colors (the walls could not have held up a vaulted roof), and completely paved, completely sheathed with marble, as some flags and other remnants indicate, this hall could not have been without some richness of effect. Those who sat there were but the magistrates of a small city; but behind them loomed up Rome, whose vast shadow embraced and magnified everything.

At length we have before us the Pantheon, the strangest and the least easy to name of the edifices of Pompeii. It is not parallel to the Forum, but its obliquity was adroitly masked by shops in which many pieces of coin have been found. Hence the conclusion that these were *tabernæ argentariæ*, the money-changers' offices, and I cannot prove the contrary. The two entrance doors are separated by two Corinthian columns, between which is hollowed out a

niche without a statue. The capitals of these columns
bear Cæsarean eagles. Could this Pantheon have
been the temple of Augustus? Having passed the
doors, one reaches an area, in which extended, to the
right and to the left, a spacious portico surrounding a
court, in the midst of which remain twelve pedestals
that, ranged in circular order, once, perhaps, sustained
the pillars of a circular temple or the statues of twelve
gods. This, then, was the Pantheon. However, at
the extremity of the edifice, and directly opposite to
the entrance, three apartments open. The middle one
formed a chapel; three statues were found there representing Drusus and Livia, the wife of Augustus, along
with an arm holding a globe, and belonging, no doubt,
to the consecrated statue which must have stood upon
the pedestal at the end, a statue of the Emperor. Then
this was the temple of Augustus. The apartment to
the left shows a niche and an altar, and served, perhaps, for sacrifices; the room to the right offers a stone
bench arranged in the shape of a horse-shoe. It could
not be one of those triple beds (*triclinia*) which we
shall find in the eating saloons of the private houses;
for the slope of these benches would have forced the

ıeclining guests to have their heads turned toward the wall or their feet higher than their heads. Moreover, in the interior of this bench runs a conduit evidently intended to afford passage to certain liquids, perhaps to the blood of animals slaughtered in the place. This, therefore, was neither a Pantheon nor a temple of Augustus, but a slaughterhouse (*macellum.*) In that case, the eleven apartments abutting to the right on the long wall of the edifice would be the stalls. But these rooms, in which the regular orifices made in the wall were to hold the beams that sustained the second story, were adorned with paintings which still exist, and which must have been quite luxurious for those poor oxen. Let us interrogate these paintings and those of all these walls; they will instruct us, perhaps, with reference to the destination of the building. There are mythological and epic pieces reproducing certain sacred subjects, of which we shall speak further cn. Others show us winged infants, little Cupids weaving garlands, of which the ancients were so fond; some of the bacchanalian divinities, celebrating the festival of the mills, are crowning with flowers the patient ass

who is turning the wheel. Flowers on all sides —
that was the fantasy of antique times. Flowers at
their wild banquets, at their august ceremonies,
at their sacrifices, and at their festivals; flowers on
the necks of their victims and their guests, and on
the brows of their women and their gods. But the
greatest number of these paintings appear destined
for banquetting-halls; dead nature predominates in
them; you see nothing but pullets, geese, ducks, part-
ridges, fowls, and game of all kinds, fruits, and eggs,
amphoræ, loaves of bread and cakes, hams, and I
know not what all else. In the shops attached to this
palace belong all sorts of precious articles—vases,
lamps, statuettes, jewels, a handsome alabaster cup;
besides, there have been found five hundred and fifty
small bottles, without counting the goblets, and, in
vases of glass, raisins, figs, chestnuts, lentils, and near
them scales and bakers' and pastry-cooks' moulds.
Could the Pantheon, then, have been a tavern, a free
inn (*hospitium*) where strangers were received under
the protection of the gods? In that case the supposed
butcher-shop must have been a sort of office, and the
triclinium a dormitory. However that may be, the

table and the altar, the kitchen and religion, elbow each other in this strange palace. Our austerity revolts and our frivolity is amused at the circumstance; but Catholics of the south are not at all surprised at it. Their mode of worship has retained something of the antique gaiety. For the common people of Naples, Christmas is a festival of eels, Easter a revel of *casatelli;* they eat *zeppole* to honor Saint Joseph; and the greatest proof of affliction that can be given to the dying Saviour is not to eat meat. Beneath the sky of Italy dogmas may change, but the religion will always be the same — sensual and vivid, impassioned and prone to excess, essentially and eternally Pagan, above all adoring woman, Venus or Mary, and the *bambino*, that mystic Cupid whom the poets called the first love. Catholicism and Paganism, theories and mysteries; if there be two religions, they are that of the south and that of the north.

You have just explored the whole eastern part of the Forum. Pass now in front of the temple of Jupiter and reach the western part. In descending from north to south, the first monument that strikes your attention is a rather long portico, turned on the east toward the Forum. Different observers have fancied that they discovered in it a *poecile*, a museum, a divan, a club, a granary for corn; and all these opinions are equally good.

Behind the poecile open small chambers, of which some are vaulted. Skeletons were found in them, and the inference was that they were prisons. Lower down extends along the Forum the lateral wall of the temple of Venus. In this wall is hollowed a small square niche in which there rose, at about a yard in height from the soil, a sort of table of tufa, indented with regular cavities, which are ranged in the order of their capacity; these were the public measures. An inscription gives us the names of the duumvirs who had gauged them by order of the decurions. As M. Breton has well remarked, they were the standards of measurement. Of these five cavities, the two smallest were destined for liquids, and we still see the holes through which those liquids flowed off when they had been measured. The table of tufa has been taken to the museum, and in its place has been substituted a rough imitation, which gives a sufficient idea of this curious monument.

The temple of Venus is entered from the neighboring street which we have already traversed. The ruin
is a fine one — the finest, perhaps, in Pompeii; a spacious inclosure, or peribolus, framing a portico of
forty-eight columns, of which many are still standing,
and the portico itself surrounding the podium, where
rose the temple — properly speaking, the house of the
goddess. In front of the entrance, at the foot of the
steps that ascend to the podium, rises the altar, poorly
calculated for living sacrifices and seemingly destined
for simple offerings of fruit, cakes, and incense, which
were consecrated to Venus. Besides the form of the
altar, an inscription found there and a statue of the
goddess, whose modest attitude recalls the masterpiece
of Florence, sufficiently authorize the name, in the absence of more exact information, that has been given
to this edifice. Others, however, have attributed it to
the worship of Bacchus; others again to that of Diana,
and the question has not yet been settled by the savans; but Venus being the patroness of Pompeii,
deserved the handsomest temple in the little city.

The columns of the peribolus or inclosure bear the
traces of some bungling repairs made between the

earthquake of 63 and the eruption of 79. They were Doric, but the attempt was to render them Corinthian, and, to this end, they were covered with stucco and topped with capitals that are not becoming to them. Against one of these columns still leans a statue in the form of a Hermes. Around the court is cut a small kennel to carry off the rain water, which was then caught in reservoirs. The wall along the Forum was gaily decorated with handsome paintings; one of these, probably on wood, was burned in the eruption, and the vacant place where it belonged is visible. Behind the temple open rooms formerly intended for the priests; handsome paintings were found there, also — among them a Bacchus, resting his elbow on the shoulder of old Silenus, who is playing the lyre. Absorbed in this music, he forgets the wine in his goblet, and lets it fall out upon a panther crouching at his feet.

We now have only to visit the temple itself, the house of the goddess. The steps that scaled the basement story were thirteen — an odd number — so that in ascending the first step with the right foot, the level of the sanctuary was also reached with the right foot. The temple was *peripterous,* that is to say, entirely

surrounded with open columns with Corinthian capi
tals. The portico opened broadly, and a mosaic of
marbles, pleasingly adjusted, formed the pavement of
the *cella*, of which the painted walls represented simple panels, separated here and there by plain pilasters. Our Lady of Pompeii dwelt there.

The last monument of the Forum on the south-
west side is the Basilica; and the street by which we
have entered separates it from the temple of Venus.
The construction of the edifice leaves no doubt
as to its destination, which is, moreover, confirmed
by the word *Basilica* or *Basilaca*, scratched here
and there by loungers with the points of their knives,
on the wall. *Basilica* — derived from a Greek word
which signifies *king* — might be translated with sufficient exactness by *royal court*. At Rome, these
edifices were originally mere covered market-places
sheltered from the rain and the sun. At a later
period, colonnades divided them in three, sometimes
even into five naves, and the simple niche which,
intended for the judges' bench, was hollowed out
at the foot of its monuments, finally developed into
a vaulted semicircle. At last, the early Christians

finding themselves crowded in the old temples, chose
the high courts of justice to therein celebrate the
worship of the new God, and the Roman Basilica
imposed its architecture and its proportions upon the
Catholic Cathedral. In the semicircle, then, where
once the ancient magistracy held its justice seat,
arose the high altar and the consecrated image of
the crucified Saviour.

The Basilica of Pompeii presents to the Forum
six pillars, between which five portals slid along
grooves which are still visible. A vestibule, or sort
of chalcidicum extends between these five entrances
and five others, indicated by two columns and four
pillars. The vestibule once crossed, the edifice appears in its truly Roman grandeur; at first glance
the eye reconstructs the broad brick columns, regu-
larly truncated in shape (they might be considered
unfinished), which are still erect on their bases and
which, crowned with Ionic volutes, were to form
a monumental portico along the four sides of this
majestic area paved with marble. Half columns
fixed in the lateral walls supported the gallery; they
joined each other in the angles; the middle space

must have been uncovered. Fragments of statues and even of mounted figures proclaim the magnificence of this monument, at the extremity of which there rose, at the height of some six feet above the soil, a tribune adorned with half a dozen Corin thian columns and probably destined for the use of the duumvirs. The middle columns stood more widely apart in order that the magistrates might, from their seats, command a view of the entire Basilica. Under this tribune was concealed a mysterious cellar with barred windows. Some antiquaries affirm that there was the place where prisoners were tortured. They forget that in Rome, in the antique time, cases were adjudged publicly before the free people.

Some of the walls of the Basilica were covered with *graphites*, that is to say, with inscriptions scratched with the point of a nail or of a knife by loungers on the way. I do not here copy the thousand and one insignificant inscriptions which I find in my rambles. They would teach us nothing but the names of the Pompeian magistrates who had constructed or reconstructed this or that monument or such-and-such a portion of an edifice with the public money. But the graphites of the Basilica merit a moment's attention. Sometimes, these are verses of Ovid or of Virgil or Propertius (never of Horace, singular to say), and frequently with curious variations. Thus, for example:

> "Quid pote durum *Saxso* aut quid mollius unda?
> Dura tamen molli *Saxsa* cavantur aqua."
>
> (*Ovid.*)

Notice the *s* in the *saxo* and the *quid pote* instead of *quid magis;* it is a Greekism.

Elsewhere were written these two lines:

> "Quisquis amator erit Scythiæ licet ambulet oris:
> Nemo adeo ut feriat barbarus esse volet."

Propertius had put this distich in an elegy in which he narrated a nocturnal promenade between Rome and Tibur. Observe the word *Scythiæ* instead of *Sycthicis*, and especially, *feriat*, which is the true reading,—the printed texts say *noceat*. Thus an excellent correction has been preserved for us by Vesuvius.

Here are other lines, the origin of which is unknown:

> "Scribenti mi dictat Amor, monstrat que Cupido
> Ah peream, sine te si Deus esse velim!"

How many modern poets have uttered the same exclamation! They little dreamed that a Pompeian, a slave no doubt, had, eighteen centuries before their time, scratched it with a nail upon the wall of a basilica. Here is a sentence that mentions gold. It has been carried out by the English poet, Wordsworth:

> "Minimum malum fit contemnendo maximum,
> Quod, crede mi, non contemnendo, erit minus."

Let us copy also this singular truth thrown into hyme by some gourmand who had counted without s host:

> " Quoi perna cocta est, si convivæ adponitur,
> Non gustat pernam, lingit ollam aut caccabum."

This *quoi* is for *cui;* the caccabus was the kettle in which the fowl was cooked.

Here follows some wholesome advice for the health of lovers:

> " Quisquis amat calidis non debet fontibus uti:
>   Nam nemo flammis ustus amare potest."

I should never get through were I to quote them all. But how many short phrases there are that, scratched here and there, cause this old monument to spring up again, by revealing the thoughts and fancies of the loungers and passers-by who peopled it so many years ago.

A lover had written this:

> " Nemo est bellus nisi qui amavit."

A friend:

> " Vale, Messala, fac me ames."

A superlative wag, but incorrect withal:

> " Cosmus nequitiae est magnussimae."

A learned man, or a philosopher:

> " Non est exsilium ex patria sapientibus."

A complaining suitor:

> " Sara non belle facis.
>   Solum me relinquis,
>   Debilis .   .   .   ."

A wrangler and disputant threatening the other party with a law-suit :

"Somius *Corneilio* (Cornelio) jus *pendre* (perendie ?) "

A sceptic who cherishes no illusions as to the mode of administering justice :

" Quod pretium legi ? "

A censor, perhaps a Christian, who knew the words addressed by the Jews to the blind man who was cured :

" Pyrrhus Getae conlegae salutem.
Moleste fero quod audivi te mortuom (sic).
Itaque vale."

A jovial wine bibber :

" Suavis vinari sitit, rogo vas valde sitit."*

A wit :

"Zetema mulier ferebat filium simulem sui nec meus erat, nec mi simulat; sed vellem esset meus, et ego volebam ut meus esset."

Tennis-players scribble :

"Amianthus, Epaphra, Tertius ludant cum Hedysio, Iucundus Nolanus petat, numeret Citus et Stacus Amianthus."

* For *sitiat*.

Wordsworth remarks that these two names, Tertius and Epaphras, are found in the epistles of St. Paul. Epaphras (in Latin, Epaphra; the suppressed letter *s* shows that this Pompeian was merely a slave) is very often named on the walls of the little city; he is accused, moreover, of being beardless or destitute of hair (*Epaphra glaber est*), and of knowing nothing about tennis. (*Epaphra pilicrepus non es*). This inscription was found all scratched over, probably by the hand of Epaphras himself, who had his own feelings of pride as a fine player.

Thus it is that the stones of Pompeii are full of revelations with reference to its people. The Basilica is easy to reconstruct and provide with living occupants. Yonder duumviri, up between the Corinthian columns; in front of them the accused; here the crowd; lovers confiding their secrets to the wall; thinkers scribbling their maxims on them; wags getting off their witticisms in the same style; the slaves, in fine, the poor, announcing to the most remote posterity that they had, at least, the game of tennis to console them for their abject condition! Still three small apartments the extremity of which rounded off into semicircles (probably inferior tribunes where subordinate magistrates, such as commissioners or justices of the peace, had their seats); then the school of Verna, cruelly dilapidated; finally a small triumphal arch on which there stood, perhaps, a *quadriga*, or four-yoked chariot-team; some pedestals of statues erected to illustrious Pompeians, to Pansa, to Sallust, to Marcus Lucretius, Decidamius Rufus; some inscriptions in honor of this one or that one, of the great Romulus, of the aged Æneas,—when all these have been seen, or glanced at, at least, you will have made the tour of the Forum.

You now know what the public exchange was in a Roman city; a spacious court surrounded by the most important monuments (three temples, the bourse, the tribunals, the prisons, etc.), inclosed on all sides (traces of the barred gates are still discernible at the entrances), adorned with statues, triumphal arches, and colonnades; a centre of business and pleasure; a place for sauntering and keeping appointments; the Corso, the Boulevard of ancient times, or in other words, the heart of the city. Without any great effort of the imagination, all this scene revives again and becomes filled with a living, variegated throng,—the portico and its

6*

two stories of columns along the edge of the reconstructed monuments; women crowd the upper galleries; loiterers drag their feet along the pavement; the
long robes gather in harmonious folds; busy merchants
hurry to the Chalcidicum; the statues look proudly
down from their re-peopled pedestals; the noble language of the Romans resounds on all sides in scanned,
sonorous measure; and the temple of Jupiter, seated at
the end of the vista, as on a throne, and richly adorned
with Corinthian elegance, glitters in all its splendor
in the broad sunshine.

An air of pomp and grandeur — a breath of Rome
--has swept over this collection of public edifices.
Let us descend from these heights and walk about
through the little city.

III.

THE STREET.

You have no need of me for this excursion. Cast a glance at the plan, and you will be able to find your own way. You will there see an oval inclosure, a wall pierced with several entrances designated by the names of the roads which ran from them, or rather of the cities at which these roads terminated — Herculaneum, Nola, Stabiæ, etc. Two-thirds of the egg are still immaculate; you discover a black spot only on the extreme right, marking out the Amphitheatre. All this white space shows you the part of Pompeii that has not yet been designated. It is a hillside covered with vineyards, gardens, and orchards. It is only on the left that you will find the lines marking the streets, the houses, the monuments, and the public squares. The text gives us the fancied names attributed to the streets, namely: the Street of Abundance, the Street of Twelve Gods, the Street of Mercury, the Street of Fortune, the Street of Fortunata, Modest Street, etc. The names given to the houses are still more arbitrary. Most of them were christened, under the old system, by the august or illustrious personages before whom they were dug out for the first time. Thus, we have at Pompeii the house of Francis II., that of Championnet, that of Joseph II.; those of the Queen of England, the King of Prussia, the Grand Duke of Tuscany; that of the Emperor, and those of the Empress and of the Princes of Russia; that of Goethe, of the Duchess de Berry, of the Duke d'Aumale — I skip them by scores. The whole Gotha Almanac might there be passed in review. This determined, ramble through the streets at will, without troubling yourself about their names, as these change often at the caprice of antiquaries and their guides.

The narrowness of these streets will surprise you; and if you come hither to look for a Broadway, you had better have remained at home. What we call great arteries of traffic were unknown to the Pompeians, who cut only small paved paths between their houses — for the sake of health, they said. We entertain different views of this question of salubrity.

The greatest width of a Pompeian street is seven yards, and there are some which are comprised, sidewalks and all, within a space of two yards and a half. These sidewalks are raised, very narrow, and paved very variously, according to the wealth or the fancy of the proprietors, who had to keep them in good order. Here are handsome stone flags; further on merely the soil beaten down; in front of the next house are marble slabs, and here and there patches of *opus signinum*, a sort of rudimentary mosaic, to which we shall refer further on. These sidewalks were intersected with curbstones, often pierced with holes — in front of shops, for instance — perhaps for tethering the cows and donkeys of the peasants who every morning brought the citizens milk or baskets of vegetables to their own doors. Between the sidewalks was hollowed out the street, paved with coarse blocks of lava which time has not worn down. When

Pansa went to the dwelling of Paratus his sandals trod the same stones that now receive the impress of our boots. On rainy days this street must have been the bed of a torrent, as the alleys and by-ways of Naples are still; hence, one, sometimes three, thicker blocks were placed so as to enable foot passengers to cross with dry feet. These small fording blocks must have made it difficult for vehicles to get by; hence, the ruts that are still found traceable on the pavement are the marks of wagons drawn slowly by oxen, and not of those light chariots which romance-writers launch forth so briskly in the ancient city. Moreover, it has been ascertained that the Pompeians went afoot; only the quality had themselves drawn about in chariots in the country. Where could room have been found for stables and carriage-houses in those dwellings scarcely larger than your hat? It was in the suburbs only, in the outskirts of the city, that the dimensions of the residences rendered anything of the kind possible. Let us, then, obliterate these chariots from our imagination, if we wish to see the streets of Pompeii as they really were.

After a shower, the rain water descended, little by little, into the gutters, and from the latter, by holes still visible, into a subterranean conduit that carried it outside of the city. One of these conduits is still open in the Street of Stabiæ, not far from the temple of Isis.

As to the general aspect of these ancient thorough-fares, it would seem dull enough, were we to represent the scene to our fancy with the houses closed, the windows gone, the dwellings with merely a naked wall for a front, and receiving air and light only from the two courts. But it was not so, as everything goes to prove. In the first place, the shops looked out on the street and were, indeed almost entirely open, like our own, offering to the gaze of the passers-by a broad counter, leaving only a small space free to the left or the right to let the vendors pass in and out. In these counters, which were usually covered with a marble slab, were hollowed the cavities wherein the grocers and liquor-dealers kept their eatables and drinkables. Behind the counters and along the walls were stone shelves, upon which the stock was put away. Fes-

toons of edibles hung displayed from pillar to pillar;
stuffs, probably, adorned the fronts, and the customers, who made their purchases from the sidewalk,
must have everywhere formed noisy and very ani-
mated groups. The native of the south gesticulates
a great deal, likes to chaffer, discusses with vehe-
mence, and speaks loudly and quickly with a glib
tongue and a sonorous voice. Just take a look at
him in the lower quarters of Naples, which, in
more than one point of view, recall the narrow
streets of Pompeii.

These shops are now dismantled. Nothing of them
remains but the empty counters, and here and there
the grooves in which the doors slid to and fro.
These doors themselves were but a number of shut-
ters fitting into each other. But the paintings or
carvings which still exist upon some side pillars
are old signs that inform us what was sold on the
adjoining counter. Thus, a goat in terra cotta indicated a milk-depot; a mill turned by an ass
showed where there was a miller's establishment;
two men, walking one ahead of the other and each
carrying one end of a stick, to the middle of which

an amphora is suspended, betray the neighborhood of a wine-merchant. Upon other pillars are marked other articles not so readily understood,—here an anchor, there a ship, and in another place a checker-board. Did they understand the game of Palamedes at Pompeii? A shop near the Thermæ, or public warm baths, is adorned on its front with a representation of a gladiatorial combat. The author of the painting thought something of his work, which he protected with this inscription: "*Abiat (habeat) Venerem Pompeianam iradam (iratam) qui hoc læserit!* (May he who injures this picture have the wrath of the Pompeian Venus upon him!)"

Other shops have had their story written by the articles that they contained when they were found. Thus, when there were discovered in a suite of rooms opening on the Street of Herculaneum, certain levers one of which ended in the foot of a pig, along with hammers, pincers, iron rings, a wagon-spring, the felloe of a wheel, one could say without being too bold that there had been the shop of a wagon-maker or blacksmith. The forge occupied only one apartment, behind which opened a

7

bath-room and a store-room. Not far from there a pottery is indicated by a very curious oven, the vault of which is formed of hollow tubes of baked clay, inserted one within the other. Elsewhere was discovered the shop of the barber who washed, brushed, shaved, clipped, combed and perfumed the Pompeians living near the Forum. The benches of masonry are still seen where the customers sat. As for the dealers in soap, unguents, and essences, they must have been numerous; their products supplied not only the toilet of the ladies, but the religious or funeral ceremonies, and after having perfumed the living, they embalmed the dead. Besides the shops in which the excavators have come suddenly upon a stock of fatty and pasty substances, which, perhaps, were soaps, we might mention one, on the pillar of which three paintings, now effaced, repre- sented a sacrificial attendant leading a bull to the altar, four men bearing an enormous chest around which were suspended several vases; then a body washed and anointed for embalming. Do you under- stand this mournful-looking sign? The unguent dealer, as he was. called, thus *made up* the body and publicly placarded it.

From the perfumery man to the chemist is but a step. The shop of the latter tradesman was found— so it is believed, at all events in clearing out a triple furnace with walled boilers. Two pharmacies or drug-stores, one in the Street of Herculaneum, the other fronting the Chalcidicum, have been more exactly designated not only by a sign on which there was seen a serpent (one of the symbols of Æscula- pius) eating a pineapple, but by tablets, pills, jars, and vials containing dried-up liquids, and a bronze med- icine chest divided into compartments which must have contained drugs. A groove for the spatula had been ingeniously constructed in this curious little piece of furniture.

Not far from the apothecary lived the doctor, who was an apothecary himself and a surgeon besides, and it was in his place that were discovered the celebrated instruments of surgery which are at the museum, and which have raised such stormy debates between Dr. Purgon and Dr. Pancratius. The first, being a doctor, deemed himself competent to give an account of these instruments, whereat the second, being an antiquary, became greatly irritated, seeing that the faculty, in his opinion, has nothing to do with archæology. However that may be, the articles are at the museum, and everybody can look at them. There is a forceps, to pull teeth with, as some affirm; to catch and compress arteries, as others declare; there is a specillum of bronze, a probe rounded in the form of an S; there are lancets, pincers, spatulæ, hooks, a trident, needles of all kinds, incision knives, cauteries, cupping-glasses—I don't know what not — fully three hundred different articles, at all events. This rich collection proves that the ancients were quite skilful in surgery and had invented many instruments thought to be modern. This is all that it is worth our while to know. For more ample information, examine the volume entitled *Memoires de l'Academie d'Herculaneum.*

Other shops (that of the color merchant, that of the goldsmith, the sculptor's atelier, etc.) have revealed to us some of the processes of the ancient artists. We know, for instance, that those of Pompeii employed mineral substances almost exclusively in the preparation of their colors; among them chalk, ochre, cinnabar, minium, etc. The vegetable kingdom furnished them nothing but lamp-black, and the animal kingdom their purple. The colors mixed with rosin have occasioned the belief that encaustic was the process used by the ancients in their mural paintings, an opinion keenly combatted by other hypotheses, themselves no less open to discussion; into this debate it is not our part to enter. However the case may be, the color dealer's family was fearfully decimated by the eruption, for fourteen skeletons were found in his shop.

As for the sculptor, he was very busy at the time of the catastrophe; quite a number of statues were found in his place blocked out or unfinished, and with them were instruments of his profession, such as scissors, punchers, files, etc. All of these are at the museum in Naples.

There were artists, then, in Pompeii, but above all, there were artisans. The fullers so often mentioned by the inscriptions must have been the most numerous; they formed a respectable corporation. Their factory has been discovered. It is a peri-

7*

style surrounded with rooms, some of which served
for shops and others for dwellings. A painted inscription on the street side announces that the dyers
(*offectores*) vote for Posthumus Proculus. These
offectores were those who retinted woollen goods.
Those who did the first dyeing were called the *infectores*. *Infectores qui alienum colorem in lanam
conficiunt, offectores qui proprio colori novum offi-
ciunt.* In the workshop there were four large basins, one above the other; the water descended from
the first to the next one and so on down to the
last, there being a fifth sunken in the ground.
Along the four basins ran a platform, at the end
of which were ranged six or seven smaller basins,
or vats, in which the stuffs were piled up and fulled.
At the other extremity of the court, a small marble reservoir served, probably, as a washing vat for
the workmen. But the most curious objects among
the ruins were the paintings, now transferred to the
museum at Naples, which adorned one of the pillars of the court. There a workman could be very
distinctly seen dressing, with a sort of brush or card,
a piece of white stuff edged with red, while another

is coming toward him, bearing on his head one of those large osier cages or frames on which the girls of that region still spread their clothes to dry. These cages resemble the bell-shaped steel contrivances which our ladies pass under their skirts. Thus, in the Neapolitan dialect, both articles are called drying-horses (*asciutta-panni*). Upon the drying-horse of the Pompeian picture perches the bird of Minerva, the protectress of the fullers and the goddess of labor. To the left of the workmen, a young girl is handing some stuffs to a youthful, richly-dressed lady, probably a customer, seated near by. Another painting represents workmen dressing and fulling all sorts of tissues, with their hands and feet in tubs or vats exactly like the small basins which we saw in the court. A third painting shows the mistress of the house giving orders to her slaves; and the fourth represents a fulling press which might be deemed modern, so greatly does it resemble those still employed in our day. The importance of this edifice, now so stripped and dilapidated, confirms what writers have told us of the Pompeian fullers and their once-celebrated branch of trade.

However, most of the shops the use of which has not
been precisely designated, were places where provisions
of different kinds were kept and sold. The oil merchant in the street leading to the Odeon was especially
noticeable among them all for the beauty of his counter, which was covered with a slab of *cipollino* and gray
marble, encrusted, on the outside, with a round slab of
porphyry between two rosettes. Eight earthenware
vases still containing olives* and coagulated oil were
found in the establishment of this stylish grocer.

The bathing concerns were also very numerous.
They were the coffee-houses of the ancient day. Hot
drinks were sold there, boiled and perfumed wine, and
all sorts of mixtures, which must have been detestable,
but for which the ancients seem to have had a special
fancy. " A thousand and a thousand times more
respectable than the wine-shops of our day, these
bathing-houses of ages gone by, where men did not

* These olives which, when found, were still soft and pasty, had
a rancid smell and a greasy but pungent flavor. The kernels were
less elongated and more bulging than those of the Neapolitan
olives; were very hard and still contained some shreds of their
pith. In a word, they were perfectly preserved, and although
eighteen centuries old, as they were, you would have thought they
had been plucked but a few months before.

assemble to shamefully squander their means and their existence while gorging themselves with wine, but where they came together to amuse themselves in a decent manner, and to drink warm water without risk." . . . . Le Sage, who wrote the foregoing sen-tence, was not accurately informed. The liquors sold at the Pompeian bathing-houses were very strong, and, in more than one place where the points of the ampho-rae rested, they have left yellow marks on the pave-ment. Vinegar has been detected in most of these drinks. In the tavern of Fortunata, the marble of the counter is still stained with the traces of the ancient goblets.

Bakeries were not lacking in Pompeii. The most complete one is in the Street of Herculaneum, where it fills a whole house, the inner court of which is occu-pied with four mills. Nothing could be more crude and elementary than those mills. Imagine two huge blocks of stone representing two cones, of which the upper one is overset upon the other, giving every mill the appearance of an hour-glass. The lower stone remained motionless, and the other revolved by means of an apparatus kept in motion by a man or a donkey.

The grain was crushed between the two stones in the old patriarchal style. The poor ass condemned to do this work must have been a very patient animal; but what shall we say of the slaves often called in to fill his place? For those poor wretches it was usually a punishment, as their eyes were put out and then they were sent to the mill. This was the menace held over their heads when they misbehaved. For others it was a very simple piece of service which more than one man of mind performed — Plautus, they say, and Terence. To some again, it was, at a later period, a method of paying for their vices; when the millers lacked hands they established bathing-houses around their mills, and the passers-by who were caught in the trap had to work the machinery.

Let us hasten to add that the work of the mill which we visited was not performed by a Christian, as they would say at Naples, but by a mule, whose bones were found in a neighboring room, most likely a stable, the racks and troughs of which were elevated about two and a half feet above the floor. In a closet near by, the watering trough is still visible. Then again, religion, which everywhere entered into the ancient manners and customs of Italy, as it does into the new, reveals itself in the paintings of the *pistrinum;* we there see the sacrifices to Fornax, the patroness of ovens and the saint of kitchens.

But let us return to our mills. Mills driven by the wind were unknown to the ancients, and water-mills did not exist in Pompeii, owing to the lack of running water. Hence these mills put in motion by manual labor—the old system employed away back in the days of Homer. On the other hand, the institution of complete baking as a trade, with all its dependent processes, did not date so far back. The primitive Romans made their bread in their own houses. Rome was already nearly five hundred years old when the first bakers established stationary mills, to which the proprietors sent their grain, as they still do in the Neapolitan provinces; in return they got loaves of bread; that is to say, their material ground, kneaded, and baked. The Pompeian establishment that we visited was one of these complete bakeries.

We could still recognize the troughs that served for the manipulation of the bread, and the oven, the arch of which is intact, with the cavity that retained the ashes, the vase for water to besprinkle the crust and make it shiny, and, finally, the triple-flued pipe that carried off the smoke — an excellent system revealed by the Pompeian excavations and successfully imitated since then. The bake-oven opened upon two small rooms by two apertures. The loaves went in at one of these in dough, and came out at the other, baked. The whole thing is in such a perfect state of preservation that one might be tempted to employ these old bricks, that have not been used for eighteen centuries, for the same purpose. The very loaves have survived. In the bakery of which I speak several were found with the stamps upon them, *siligo grani* (wheat flour), or *e cicera* (of bean flour) — a wise precaution against the bad faith of the dealers. Still more recently, in the latest excavations, Signor Fiorelli came across an oven so hermetically sealed that there was not a particle of ashes in it, and there were eighty-one loaves, a little sad, to be sure, but whole, hard, and black, found in the order in which they had been placed on the 23d of November, 79. Enchanted with this windfall, Fiorelli himself climbed into the oven and took out the precious relics with his own hands.

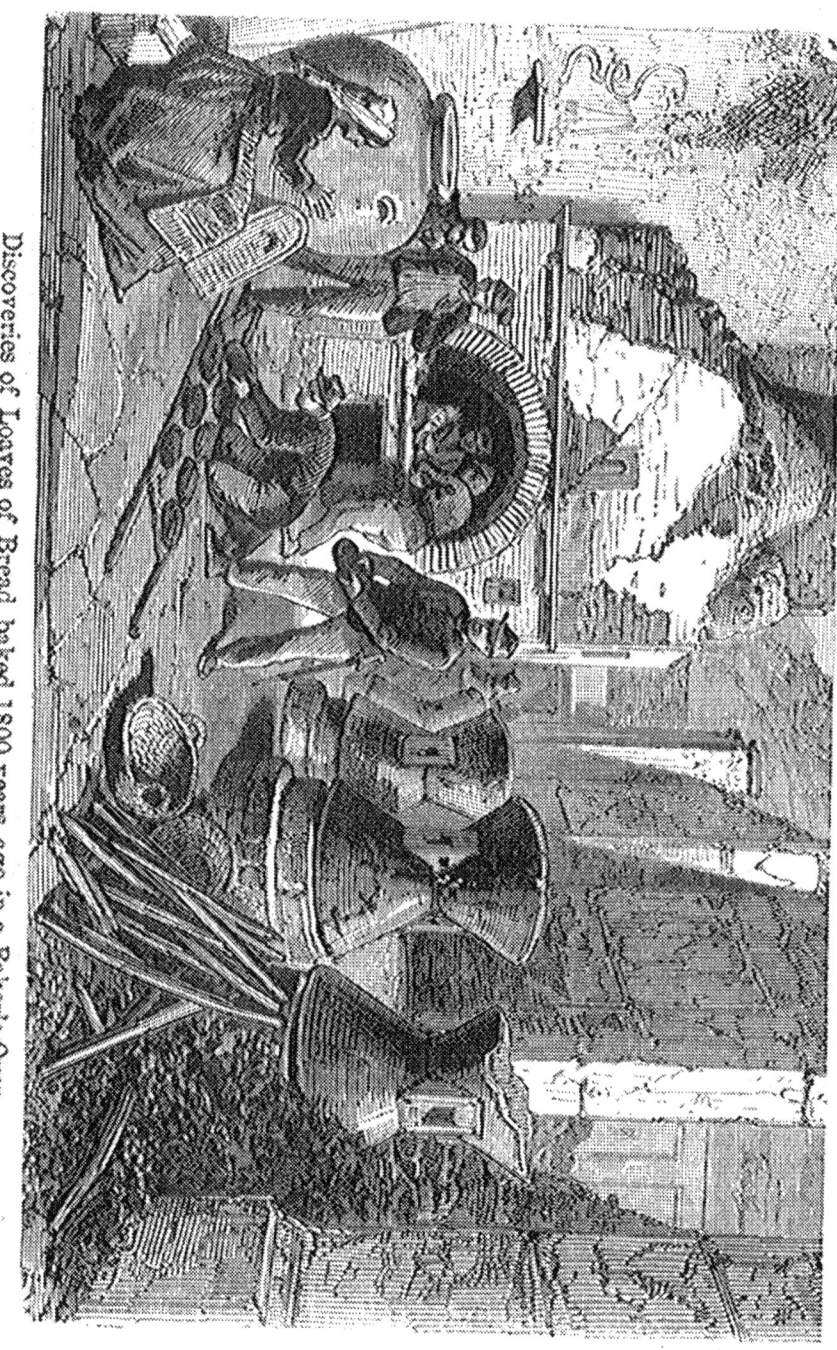

Discoveries of Loaves of Bread baked 1800 years ago in a Baker's Oven.

Most of the loaves weigh about a pound; the heaviest
twelve hundred and four grains. They are round,
depressed in the centre, raised on the edges, and
divided into eight lobes. Loaves are still made in
Sicily exactly like them. Professor de Luca weighed
and analyzed them minutely, and gave the result in
a letter addressed to the French Academy of Sciences.
Let us now imagine all these salesrooms, all these
shops, open and stocked with goods, and then the dis-
play, the purchasers, the passers-by, the bustle and noise
peculiar to the south, and the street will no longer seem
so dead. Let us add that the doors of the houses were
closed only in the evening; the promenaders and
loungers could then peep, as they went along, into
every alley, and make merry at the bright adornments of the *atrium.* Nor is this all. The upper
stories, although now crumbled to dust, were in
communication with the street. Windows opened
discreetly, which must, here and there, have been
the framework of some brown head and countenance
anxious to see and to be seen. The latest excavations have revealed the existence of hanging covered
balconies, long exterior corridors, pierced with case-

8

ments, frequently depicted in the paintings. There the fair Pompeian could have taken her station in order to participate in the life outside. The good housewife of those times, like her counterpart in our day, could there have held out her basket to the street-merchant who went wandering about with his portable shop; and more than one handsome girl may at the same post have carried her fingers to her lips, there to cull (the ancient custom) the kiss that she flung to the young Pompeian concealed down yonder in the corner of the wall. Thus re-peopled, the old-time street, narrow as it is, was gayer than our own thoroughfares; and the brightly-painted houses, the variegated walls, the monuments, and the fountains, gave vivid animation to a picture too dazzling for our gaze.

These fountains, which were very simple, consisted of large square basins formed of five stone slabs, one for the bottom and four for the sides, fastened to-gether with iron braces. The water fell into them from fonts more or less ornamental and usually repre-senting the muzzle of some animal — lions' heads, masks, an eagle holding a hare in his beak, with

Closed House with a Balcony, recently discovered.

the stream flowing into a receptacle from the hare's mouth. One of these fountains is surrounded with an iron railing to prevent passers-by from falling into it. Another is flanked by a capacious vaulted reservoir (*castellum*) and closed with a door. Those who have seen Rome know how important the ancients considered the water that they brought from a distance by means of the enormous aqueducts, the ruins of which still mark all the old territories of the empire. Water, abundant and limpid, ran everywhere, and was never deficient in the Roman cities. Still it has not been discovered how the supply was obtained for Pompeii, destitute of springs as that city was, and, at the same time, elevated above the river, and receiving nothing in its cisterns but the rain-water so scantily shed beneath the relentless serenity of that southern sky. The numberless conduits found, of lead, masonry, and earthenware, and above all, the spouting fountains that leaped and sparkled in the courtyards of the wealthy houses, have led us to suppose the existence of an aqueduct, no longer visible, that supplied all this part of Campania with water.

Besides these fountains, placards and posters enlivened the streets ; the walls were covered with them,
and, in sundry places, whitewashed patches of masonry
served for the announcements so lavishly made public.
These panels, dedicated entirely to the poster business,
were called *albums*. Anybody and everybody had the
right to paint thereon in delicate and slender red
letters all the advertisements which now-a-days we
print on the last, and even on many other pages of
our newspapers. Nothing is more curious than these
inscriptions, which disclose to us all the subjects enga-
ging the attention of the little city; not only its excite-
ments, but its language, ancient and modern, collegiate
and common — the Oscan, the Greek, the Latin, and the
local dialect. Were we learned, or anxious to appear
so, we could, with the works of the really erudite
(Fiorelli, Garrucci, Mommsen, etc.), to help us, have
compiled a chapter of absolutely appalling science in
reference to the epigraphic monuments of Pompeii.
We could demonstrate by what gradations the Oscan
language — that of the Pompeian autonomy — yielded
little by little to the Roman language, which was that
of the unity of the state ; and to what extent Pompeii,

which never was a Greek city, employed the sacred idiom of the divine Plato. We might even add some observations relative to the accent and the dialect of the Pompeians, who pronounced Latin as the Neapolitans pronounce Tuscan and with singularly analogous alterations. But what you are looking for here, hurried reader, is not erudition, but living movement. Choose then, in these inscriptions, those that teach us something relative to the manners and customs of this dead people — dead and buried, but afterward exhumed.

The most of these announcements are but the proclamations of candidates for office. Pompeii was evidently swallowed up at the period of the elections. Sometimes it is an elector, sometimes a group of citizens, then again a corporation of artisans or tradesmen, who are recommending for the office of ædile or duumvir the candidate whom they prefer. Thus, Paratus nominates Pansa, Philippus prefers Caius Aprasius Felix; Valentinus, with his pupils, chooses Sabinus and Rufus. Sometimes the elector is in a hurry; he asks to have his candidate elected quickly. The fruiterers, the public porters, the muleteers, the

salt-makers, the carpenters, the truckmen, also unite to
push forward the ædile who has their confidence. Frequently, in order to give more weight to its vote, the corporation declares itself unanimous.   Thus, all the gold-
smiths preferred a certain Photinus — a fishmonger,
thinks Overbeck — for ædile.   Let us not forget *the
sleepers*, who declare for Vatia.   By the way, who were
these friends of sleep?   Perhaps they were citizens
who disliked noise ; perhaps, too, some association of
nocturnal revellers thus disguised under an ironical
and reassuring title.   Sometimes the candidate is recommended by a eulogistic epithet indicated by seals,
a style of abbreviation much in use among the ancients.   The person recommended is always a good
man, a man of probity, an excellent citizen, a very
moral individual.   Sometimes positive wonders are
promised on his behalf.   Thus, after having designated
Julius Polybius for the ædileship, an elector announces that he will bring in good bread.   Electoral
intrigue went still further.   *We* are pretty well on
in that respect, but I think that the ancients were
our masters.   I read the following bare-faced avowal
on a wall: *Sabinum ædilem, Procule, fac et ille te*

faciet. (Make Sabinus ædile, O Proculus, and he may make thee such!) Frank and cool that, it strikes me!

But enough of elections; there is no lack of announcements of another character. Some of these give us the programme of the shows in the amphitheatre; such-and-such a troop of gladiators will fight on such a day; there will be hunting matches and awnings, as well as sprinklings of perfumed waters to refresh the multitude (*venatio, vela, sparsiones*). Thirty couples of gladiators will ensanguine the arena.

There were, likewise, posters announcing apartments to let.

Some of these inscriptions, either scratched or painted, were witticisms or exclamations from facetious passers-by. One ran thus: "Oppius the porter is a robber, a rogue!" Sometimes there were amorous declarations: "Augea loves Arabienus." Upon a wall in the Street of Mercury, an ivy leaf, forming a heart, contained the gentle name of Psyche. Elsewhere a wag, parodying the style of monumental inscriptions, had announced that under the consulate of L. Monius Asprenas and A. Plotius, there was born to him the foal of an ass. "A wine jar has been lost and he who brings it back shall have such a reward from Varius; but he who will bring the thief shall have twice as much."

Again, still other inscriptions were notifications to the public in reference to the cleanliness of the streets, and recalling in terms still more precise the "Commit no Nuisance" put up on the corners of some of our streets with similar intent. On more than one wall at Pompeii the figures of serpents, very well painted, sufficed to prevent any impropriety, for the serpent was a sacred symbol in ancient Rome —strange mingling of religion in the pettiest details of common life! Only a very few years ago, the Neapolitans still followed the example of their ancestors; they protected the outside walls of their dwellings with symbolical paintings, rudely tracing, not serpents, but crosses on them.

IV.

THE SUBURBS.

> "Ce qu'on trouve aux abords d'une grande cite,
>   Ce sont des abattoirs, des murs, des cimitieres ;
> C'est ainsi qu'en entrant dans la societé
>   On trouve ses egouts."

ALFRED DE MUSSET would have depicted the sub-urban quarters of Pompeii exactly in these lines, had he added to his enumeration the wine-shops and the custom-house. The latter establishment was not omitted by the ancients, and could not be forgotten in our diminutive but highly commercial city. Thus, the place has been discovered where the collector awaited the passage of the vehicles that came in from the country and the neighboring villages. Ab-solutely nothing else remains to be seen in this spa-cious mosaic-paved hall. Scales, steelyards, and a quantity of stone or metal weights were found there, marked with inscriptions sometimes quite curious; such, for example, as the following: *Eme et habbebis*, with a *b* too many, a redundancy very frequent in the Naples dialect. This is equivalent, in English, to: Buy and you will have. One of the sets of scales bears an inscription stating that it had been verified or authorized at the Capitol under such consuls and such emperors — the hand of Rome!

Besides the custom-house, this approach to the city contained abundance of stables, coach-houses, taverns, bath-houses, low drinking-shops, and other disreputable concerns. Even the dwellings in the same quarter have a suspicious look. You follow a long street and you have before you the gate of Herculaneum and the walls.

These walls are visible; they still hold firm. Unquestionably, they could not resist our modern cannon, for if the ancients built better than we do, we destroy better than they did; this is one thing that must in justice be conceded to us. Nevertheless, we cannot but admire those masses of *peperino*, the points of which ascend obliquely and hold together without mortar. Originally as ancient as the city, these ramparts were destroyed to some extent by Sylla and repaired in *opus incertum*, that is to say, in small stones of every shape and of various dimensions, fitted to one another without order or regularity in the layers, as though they had been put in just as they came. The old structure dated probably from the time of Pompeian autonomy— the Oscans had a hand in them. The surrounding wall, at the foot of which there were no ditches, would have formed an oval line of nearly two miles had it not been interrupted, on the side of the mountains and the sea, between the ports of Stabiæ and of Herculaneum. These ramparts consisted of two walls—the scarp and counterscarp,—between which ran a terraced platform; the exterior wall, slightly sloping, was defended by embrasures between which the archer could place himself in safety, in an angle of the stonework, so soon as he had shot his arrow. The interior wall was also crested with battlements. The curvilinear rampart did not present projecting angles, the salients of which, Vitruvius tells us, could not resist the repeated blows of the siege machinery

of those days. It was intersected by nine towers,
of three vaulted stories each, at unequal distances,
accordingly as the nature of the ground demanded
greater or less means of defence, was pierced with loop-
holes and was not very solid. Vitruvius would have had
them rounded and of cut stone; those of Pompeii
are of quarried stone, and in small rough ashlars,
stuck together with mortar. The third story of each‛
tower reached to the platform of the rampart, with
which it communicated by two doors.

Notwithstanding all that remains of them, the walls
of Pompeii were no longer of service at the time
of the eruption. Demolished by Sylla and then by
Augustus, shattered by the earthquake, and interrupted as I have said, they left the city open.
They must have served for a public promenade, like
the bastions of Geneva.

Eight gates opened around the city (perhaps there
was a ninth that has now disappeared, opening out
upon the sea). The most singular of all of them is
the Nola gate, the construction of which appears to
be very ancient. We there come across those fine
cut stones that reveal the handiwork of primitive

The Nola Gate at Pompeii.

times. A head consideraly broken and defaced, surmounting the arcade, was accompanied with an Oscan
inscription, which, having been badly read by a
savant, led for an instant to the belief that the Campanians of the sixth century before Jesus Christ
worshipped the Egyptian Isis. The learned inter-
preter had read: *Isis propheta* (I translate it into
Latin, supposing you to know as little as I do of the
Oscan tongue). The inscription really ran, *idem
probavit*.

It is worth while passing through the gate to get
a look at the angle formed by the ramparts at this
one point. I doubt whether the city was ever attacked on that side. Before reaching the gate the
assailants would have had to wind along through a
narrow gallery, where the archers, posted on the walls
and armed with arrows and stones, would have
crushed them all.

The Herculaneum gate is less ancient, and yet more
devastated by time than the former one. The arcade
has fallen in, and it requires some attention to rein-
state it. This gate formed three entrances. The two
side ways were probably intended for pedestrians;

the one in the middle was closed by means of a portcullis sliding in a groove, still visible, but covered with
stucco. As the portcullis, in descending, would have
thrown down this coating, we must infer that at the
time of the eruption it had not been in use for a long
while, Pompeii having ceased to be a fortified place.

The Herculaneum gate was not masked inside, so
that the archers, standing upon the terraces that covered the side entrances, could fire upon the enemy
even after the portcullis had been carried. We know
that one of the stratagems of the besieged consisted
in allowing the enemy to push in, and then suddenly
shutting down upon them the formidable *cataracta*
suspended by iron chains. They then slaughtered the
poor wretches indiscriminately and covered themselves with glory.

Having passed the gate, we find ourselves on one
of those fine paved roads which, starting at Rome in
all directions, have everywhere left very visible traces,
and in many places still serve for traffic. The Greeks
had gracefulness, the Romans grandeur. Nothing
shows this more strikingly than their magnificent
highways that pierce mountains, fill up ravines, level

The Herculaneum Gate, restored.

the plains, cross the marshes, bestride rivers, and even valleys, and stretched thus from the Tiber to the Euphrates. In order to construct them they first traced two parallel furrows, from between which they removed all the loose earth, which they replaced with selected materials, strongly packed, pressed, and pounded down. Upon this foundation (the *pavimentum*) was placed a layer of rough stone (*statumen*), then a filling-in of gravel and lime (the *rudus*), and, finally, a third bed of chalk, brick, lime, clay, and sand, kneaded and pounded in together into a solid crust. This was the nucleus. Last of all, they placed above it those large rough blocks of lava which you will find everywhere in the environs of Naples. As before remarked, these roads have served for twenty centuries, and they are good yet.

The Herculaneum road formed a delightful promenade at the gates of Pompeii; a street lined with trees and villas, like the Champs Elyseés at Paris, and descending from the city to the country between two rows of jaunty monuments prettily-adorned, niches, kiosks, and gay pavilions, from which the view was admirable. This promenade was the cemetery of

Pompeii. But let not this intimation trouble you, for nothing was less mournful in ancient times than a cemetery. The ancients were not fond of death; they even avoided pronouncing its name, and resorted to all sorts of subterfuges to avoid the doleful word. They spoke of the deceased as "those who had been," or "those who are gone." Very demonstrative, at the first moment they would utter loud lamentations. Their sorrow thus vented its first paroxysms. But the first explosion over, there remained none of that clinging melancholy or serious impression that continues in our Christian countries. The natives of the south are epicureans in their religious belief, as in their habits of life. Their cemeteries were spacious avenues, and children played jackstones on the tombs.

Would you like to hear a few details in reference to the interments of the ancients. " The usage was this," says Claude Guichard, a doctor at law, in his book concerning funereal rites, printed at Lyons, in 1581, by Jean de Tournes: "When the sick person was in extreme danger, his relatives came to see him, seated themselves on his bed, and kept him company until the death-rattle came on and his features began to assume the dying look. Then the nearest relative among them, all in tears, approached the pa tient and embraced him closely, breast against breast and face against face, so as to receive his soul, and mouth to mouth, catching his last breath; which done, he pressed together the lips and eyes of the dead man, arranging them decently, so that the persons present might not see the eyes of the deceased open, for, according to their customs, it was not allowable to the living to see the eyes of the dead. . . . Then the room was opened on all sides, and they allowed all persons belonging to the family and neighborhood, to come in, who chose. Then, three or four of them began to bewail the deceased and call to him repeatedly, and, perceiving that he did not reply one word, they went out and told of the death. Then the near relatives went to the bedside to give the last kiss to the deceased, and handed him over to the chambermaids of the house, if he was a person of the lower class. If he was one of the eminent men and heads of families, he committed him to the care of people authorized to perform this office, to wash, anoint, and dress him, in accordance with the cus-

9*

tom and what was requisite in view of the quality, greatness, and rank of the personage."

Now there were at Rome several ministers, public servitors, and officials, who had charge of all that appertained to funerals, such as the *libitinarii*, the *designatores*, and the like. All of which was wisely instituted by Numa Pompilius, as much to teach the Romans not to hold things relating to the dead in horror, or fly from them as contaminating to the person, as in order to fix in their memory that all that has had a beginning in birth must in like manner terminate in death, birth and death both being under the control and power of one and the same deity; for they deemed that Libītina was the same as Venus, the goddess of procreation. Then, again, the said officers had under their orders different classes of serfs whom they called, in their language, the *pollinctores*, the *sandapilarii*, the *ustores*, the *cadaverum custodes*, intrusted with the care of anointing the dead, carrying them to the place of sepulture, burning them, and watching them. "After the *pollinctores* had carefully washed, anointed, and embalmed the body, according to the

custom regarding it and the expense allowed, they
wrapped it in a white linen cloth, after the manner
of the Egyptians, and in this array placed it upon a
bed handsomely prepared as though for the most
distinguished member of the household, and then
raised in front of the latter a small dresser shaped
like an altar, upon which they placed the usual odors
and incense, to burn along with tapers and lighted
candles. . . . Then, if the deceased was a person
of note, they kept the body thus arranged for the
space of seven consecutive days, inside the house, and,
during that time, the near relatives, dressed in certain
long robes or very loose and roomy mantles called
ricinia, along with the chambermaids and other
women taken thither to weep, never ceased to la-
ment and bewail, renewing their distress every time
any notable personage entered the room; and they
thought that all this while the deceased remained on
earth, that is to say, kept for a few days longer at
the house, while they were hastening their prepara-
tions for the pomp and magnificence of his funeral.
On the eighth day, so as to assemble the relatives,
associates, and friends of the defunct the more easily,

inform the public and call together all who wished to be present, the procession, which they called *exequiæ*, was cried aloud and proclaimed with the sound of the trumpet on all the squares and chief places of the city by the crier of the dead, in the following form: 'Such a citizen has departed from this life, and let all who wish to be present at his obsequies know that it is time; he is now to be carried from his dwelling.'"

Let us step aside now, for here comes a funeral procession. Who is the deceased? Probably a consular personage, a duumvir, since lictors lead the line. Behind them come the flute-players, the mimes and mountebanks, the trumpeters, the tambourine-players, and the weepers (*præficæ*), paid for uttering cries, tearing their hair, singing notes of lamentation, extolling the dead man, mimicking despair, "and teaching the chambermaids how to best express their grief, since the funeral must not pass without weeping and wailing." All this makes up a melancholy but burlesque din, which attracts the crowd and swells the procession, to the great honor of the defunct. Afterward come the magistrates, the decurions in mourning robes, the bier ornamented with ivory. The duumvir Lucius Labeo (he is the person whom they are burying) is "laid out at full length, and dressed in white shrouds and rich coverings of purple, his head raised slightly and surrounded with a handsome coronet, if he merit it." Among the slaves who carry the bier walks a man whose head is covered with white wool, "or with a cap, in sign of liberty." That is the freedman Menomachus, who has grown rich, and who is conducting the mourning for his master. Then come unoccupied beds, "couches fitted up with the same draperies as that on which reposes the body of the defunct" (it is written that Sylla had six thousand of these at his funeral), then the long line of wax images of ancestors (thus the dead of old interred the newly dead), then the relatives, clad in mourning, the friends, citizens, and townsfolk generally in crowds. The throng is all the greater when the deceased is the more honored. Lastly, other trumpeters, and other pantomimists and tumblers, dancing, grimacing, gambolling, and mimicking the duumvir whom they are helping to bury, close the procession. This interminable multitude passes out into the Street of Tombs by the Herculaneum gate.

The *ustrinum,* or room in which they are going to burn the body, is open. You are acquainted with this Roman custom. According to some, it was a means of hastening the extrication of the soul from the body and its liberation from the bonds of matter, or its fusion in the great totality of things; according to others, it was but a measure in behalf of public health. However that may be, dead bodies might be either buried or burned, provided the deposit of the corpse or the ashes were made outside of the city. A part of the procession enters the *ustrinum.* Then they are going to burn the duumvir Lucius Labeo.

The funeral pyre is made of firs, vine branches, and other wood that burns easily. The near relatives and the freedman take the bier and place it conveniently on the pile, and then the man who closes the eyes of the dead opens them again, making the defunct look up toward the sky, and gives him the last kiss. Then they cover the pile with perfumes and essences, and collect about it all the articles of furniture, garments, and precious objects that they want to burn. The trumpets sound, and the freedman, taking a torch and turning away his eyes, sets fire to the framework. Then commence the sacrifices to the manes, the formalities, the pantomimic action, the howlings of the mourners, the combats of the gladiators "in order to satisfy the ceremony closely observed by them which required that human blood should be shed before the lighted pile;" this was done so effectually that when there were no gladiators the women "tore each other's hair, scratched their eyes and their cheeks with their nails, *heartily*, until the blood came, thinking in this manner to appease and propitiate the infernal deities, whom they suppose to be angered against the soul of the defunct, so as to treat it roughly, were this doleful ceremony omitted and disdained." . . . The body burned, the mother, wife, or other near relative of the dead, wrapped and clad in a black garment, got ready to gather up the relics — that is to say, the bones which remained and had not been totally consumed by the fire; and, before doing anything, invoked the deity manes, and the soul of the dead man, beseeching him to take this devotion in good part, and not to think ill of this service. Then, after having washed her hands well, and having extinguished the fire in the brazier

with wine or with milk, she began to pick out the bones
among the ashes and to gather them into her bosom
or the folds of her robe. The children also gathered
them, and so did the heirs; and we find that the
priests who were present at the obsequies could help
in this. But if it was some very great lord, the
most eminent magistrates of the city, all in silk,
ungirdled and barefooted, and their hands washed,
as we have said, performed this office themselves.
Then they put these relics in urns of earthenware,
or glass, or stone, or metal; they besprinkled them with
oil or other liquid extracts; they threw into the urn,
sometimes, a piece of coin, which sundry antiquaries
have thought was the obolus of Charon, forgetting
that the body, being burned, no longer had a hand to
hold it out; and, finally, the urn was placed in a
niche or on a bench arranged in the interior of the
tomb. On the ninth day, the family came back to
banquet near the defunct, and thrice bade him adieu:
Vale! Vale! Vale! then adding, "May the earth rest
lightly on thee!"

Hereupon, the next care was the monument.
That of the duumvir Labeo, which is very ugly, in

opus incertum, covered with stucco and adorned with bas-reliefs and portraits of doubtful taste, was built at the expense of his freedman, Menomachus. The ceremony completed and vanity satisfied, the dead was forgotten; there was no more thought, excepting for the *ferales* and *lemurales,* celebrations now retained by the Catholics, who still make a trip to the cemetery on the Day of the Dead. The Street of the Tombs, saddened for a moment, resumed its look of unconcern and gaiety, and children once more played about among the sepulchres.

There are monuments of all kinds in this suburban avenue of Pompeii. Many of them are simple pillars in the form of Hermes-heads. There is one in quite good preservation that was closed with a marble door; the interior, pierced with one window, still had in a niche an alabaster vase containing some bones. Another, upon a plat of ground donated by the city, was erected by a priestess of Ceres to her husband, H. Alleius Luceius Sibella, aedile, duumvir, and five years' prefect, and to her son, a decurion of Pompeii, deceased at the age of seventeen. A decurion at seventeen!—there was a youth who made his

10

way rapidly. Cicero said that it was easier to be a
Senator at Rome than a decurion at Pompeii. The
tomb is handsome—very elegant, indeed—but it contained neither urns, nor sarcophagi; it probably was
not a place of burial, but a simple cenotaph, an
honorary monument.

The same may be said of the handsomest mauso-
leum on the street, that of the augustal Calventius:
a marble altar gracefully decorated with arabesques
and reliefs (Œdipus meditating, Theseus reposing,
and a young girl lighting a funeral pile). Upon the
tomb are still carved the insignia of honor belonging to Calventius, the oaken crowns, the *bisellium* (a
bench with seats for two), the stool, and the three
letters O. C. S. (*ob civum servatum*), indicating that
to the illustrious dead was due the safety of a citizen
of Rome. The Street of the Tombs, it will be seen,
was a sort of Pantheon. An inscription discovered
there and often repeated (that which, under Charles
III., was the first that revealed the existence of Pompeii), informs us that, upon the order of Vespasian,
the tribune Suedius Clemens had yielded to the
commune of Pompeii the places occupied by the

private individuals, which meant that the notables only, authorized by the decurions, had the right to sleep their last slumber in this triumphal avenue, while the others had to be dispossessed. Still the hand of Rome!

Another monument—the one attributed to Scaurus —was very curious, owing to the gladiatorial scenes carved on it, and which, according to custom, represented real combats. Each figure was surmounted with an inscription indicating the name of the gladiator and the number of his victories. We know, already, that these sanguinary games formed part of the funeral ceremonies. The heirs of the deceased made the show for the gratification of the populace, either around the tombs or in the amphitheatre, whither we shall go at the close of our stroll, and where we shall describe the carvings on the pretended monument of Scaurus.

The tomb of Nevoleia Tyché, much too highly decorated, encrusted with arabesques and reliefs representing the portrait of that lady, a sacrifice, a ship (a symbol of life, say the sentimental antiquaries), is covered with a curious inscription, which I translate literally.

" Nevoleia Tyché, freedwoman of Julia, for herself
and for Caius Munatius Faustus, knight and mayor of
the suburb, to whom the decurions, with the consent
of the people, had awarded the honor of the *bisellium.*
This monument has been offered during her lifetime
by Nevoleia Tyché to her freedmen and to those of
C. Munatius Faustus."

Assuredly, after reading this inscription, we cannot
reproach the fair Pompeians with concealing their
affections from the public. Nevoleia certainly was
not the wife of Munatius ; nevertheless, she loved him
well, since she made a trysting with him even in the
tomb. It was Queen Caroline Murat who, accompanied by Canova, was the first to penetrate to the
inside of this dovecote (January 14, 1813). There
were opened in her presence several glass urns with
leaden cases, on the bottom of which still floated some
ashes in a liquid not yet dried up, a mixture of water,
wine, and oil. Other urns contained only some bones
and the small coin which has been taken for Charon's
obolus.

I have many other tombs left to mention. There
are three, which are sarcophagi, still complete, never

open, and proving that the ancients buried their dead even before Christianity prohibited the use of the funeral pyre. Families had their choice between the two systems, and burned neither men who had been struck by lightning (they thought the bodies of such to be incorruptible), nor new-born infants who had not yet cut their teeth. Thus it was that the remains of Diomed's youngest children could not be found, while those of the elder ones were preserved in a glass urn contained in a vase of lead.

A tomb that looks like a sentry-box, and stands as though on duty in front of the Herculaneum gate, had, during the eruption, been the refuge of a soldier, whose skeleton was found in it. Another strangely-decorated monument forms a covered hemi-cycle turned toward the south, fronting the sea, as though to offer a shelter for the fatigued and heated passers-by. Another, of rounded shape, presents inside a vault bestrewn with small flowers and decorated with bas-reliefs, one of which represents a female laying a fillet on the bones of her child. Other monuments are adorned with garlands. One of the least curious contained the magnificent blue and white

10*

glass vase of which I shall have to speak further on That of the priestess Mamia, ornamented with a superb inscription, forms a large circular bench terminating in a lion's claw. Visitors are fond of resting there to look out upon the landscape and the sea. Let us not forget the funereal triclinium, a simply-decorated dining-hall, where still are seen three beds of masonry, used at the banquets given in honor of the dead. These feasts, at which nothing was eaten but shell-fish (poor fare, remarks Juvenal), were celebrated nine days after the death. Hence came their title, *novendialia*. They were also called *silicernia;* and the guests conversed at them about the exploits and benevolent deeds of the man who had ceased to live. Polybius boasts greatly of these last honors paid to illustrious citizens. Thence it was, he says, that Roman greatness took its rise.

In fact, even at Pompeii, in this humble *campo santo* of the little city, we see at every step virtue rewarded after death by some munificent act of the decurions. Sometimes it is a perpetual grant (a favor difficult to obtain), indicated by the following letters: H. M. H. N. S. (*hoc monumentum hæredes non sequitur*), insuring to them the perpetual possession of their sepulchre, which could not be disposed of by their heirs. Sometimes the space conceded was indicated upon the tomb. For instance, we read in the sepulchre of the family of Nistacidius: "A. Nistacidius Helenus, mayor of the suburb Augusto-Felix. To Nistacidius Januarius and to Mesionia Satulla. Fifteen feet in depth, fifteen feet in frontage."

This bench of the priestess Mamia and that of Aulus Vetius (a military tribune and duumvir dispensing justice) were in like manner constructed, with the consent of the people, upon the lands conceded by the decurions. In fine — and this is the most singular feature — animals had their monuments. This, at least, is what the guides will tell you, as they point out a large tomb in a street of the suburbs. They call it the *sepolcro dei bestiani*, because the skeletons of bulls were found in it. The antiquaries rebel against this opinion. Some, upon the strength of the carved masks, affirm that it was a burial place for actors; others, observing that the inclosure walls shut in quite a spacious temple, intimate that it was a cemetery for priests. For my part, I have nothing to offer against the opinion of the guides. The Egyptians, whose gods Rome adopted, interred the bull Apis magnificently. Animals might, therefore, find burial in the noble suburb of Pompeii. As for the lower classes, they slept their final sleep where they could; perhaps in the common burial pit (*commune sepulcrum*), an ancient barbarism that has been kept up until our times; perhaps in those public burial ranges where one could purchase a simple niche (*olla*) for his urn. These niches were sometimes humble and touching presents interchanged by poor people.

And in this street, where death is so gay, so vain, so richly adorned, where the monuments arose amid the foliage of trees perennially green, which they had endeavored, but without success, to render serious and sombre, where the mausolea are pavilions and dining-rooms, in which the inscriptions recall whole narratives of life and even love affairs, there stood spacious inns and sumptuous villas — for instance, those of Arrius Diomed and Cicero. This Arrius Diomed was one of the freedmen of Julia, and the mayor of the suburb. A rich citizen, but with a bad heart, he left his wife and children to perish in his cellar, and fled alone with one slave only, and all the silver that he could carry away. He perished in front of his garden gate. May the earth press heavily upon him!

Ilis villa, which consisted of three stories, not placed one above the other, but descending in terraces from the top of the hill, deserves a visit or two. You will there see a pretty court surrounded with columns and small rooms, one of which — of an elliptical shape and opening on a garden, and lighted by the evening twilight, but shielded from the sun by windows and by curtains, the glass panes and rings of which have been found — is the pleasantest nook cleared out among these ruins. You will also be shown the baths, the saloons, the bedchambers, the garden, a host of small apartments brilliantly decorated, basins of marble, and the cellar still intact, with amphoræ, inside of which were still a few drops of wine not yet dried up, the place where lay the poor suffocated family — seventeen skeletons surprised there together by death. The fine ashes that stifled them having hardened with time, retain the print of a young girl's bosom. It was this strange mould, which is now kept at the museum, that inspired the *Arria Marcella* of Theophile Gau-

tier—that author's masterpiece, perhaps, but at all
events a masterpiece.

As for Cicero, get them to show you his villa, if you
choose.   You will see absolutely nothing there, and it
has been filled up again.   Fine paintings were found
there previously, along with superb mosaics and a rich
collection of precious articles; but I shall not copy the
inventory.   Was it really the house of Cicero?   Who
can say?   Antiquaries will have it so, and so be it,
then!   I do not deny that Cicero had a country
property at Pompeii, for he often mentions it in his
letters; but where it was, exactly, no one can demonstrate.   He could have descried it from Baiæ or Misenum, he somewhere writes, had he possessed longer
vision; but in such case he could also have seen the
entire side of Pompeii that looks toward the sea.
Therefore, I put aside these useless discussions and
resume our methodical tour.

I have shown you the ancients in their public life;
at the Forum and in the street, in the temples and in
the wine-shops, on the public promenade and in the
cemeteries.   I shall now endeavor to come upon them

in their private life, and, for this end, to peep at them first in a place which was a sort of intermediate point between the street and the house. I mean the hot baths, or **thermæ.**

V.

THE THERMÆ.

THE Romans were almost amphibious. They bathed themselves as often as seven times per diem; and young people of style passed a portion of the day, and often a part of the night, in the warm baths. Hence the importance which these establishments assumed in ancient times. There were eight hundred and fifty-six public baths at Rome, in the reign of Augustus. Three thousand bathers could assemble in the thermæ of Caracalla, which had sixteen hundred seats of marble or of porphyry. The thermæ of Septimius Severus, situated in a park, covered a space of one hundred thousand square feet, and comprised rooms of all kinds: gymnasia, academic halls where poets read their verses aloud, arenas for gladiators, and even theatres. Let us not forget that the Bull and the Farnese Hercules, now so greatly admired at Naples, and the masterpieces of the Vatican, the Torso at the Belvidere, and the Laocoon were found at the baths.

These immense palatial structures were accessible to everybody. The price of admission was a *quadrans*, and the *quadrans* was the fourth part of an *as;* the latter, in Cicero's time, was worth about one cent and two mills. Even this charge was afterward abolished. At daybreak, the sound of a bell announced the opening of the baths. The rich went there particularly between the middle of the day and sunset; the dissipated went after supper, in defiance of the prescribed rules of health. I learn from Juvenal, however, that they sometimes died of it. Nevertheless, Nero remained at table from noon until midnight, after which he took warm baths in winter and snow baths in summer.

In the earlier times of the republic there was a difference of hours for the two sexes. The thermæ were monopolized alternately by the men and the women, who never met there. Modesty was carried so far that the son would not bathe with his father, nor even with his father-in-law. At a later period, men and women, children and old folks, bathed pell-mell together at the public baths, until the Emperor Hadrian, recognizing the abuse, suppressed it.

Pompeii, or at least that portion of Pompeii which has been exhumed, had two public bathing establishments. The most important of these, namely, the Stabian baths, was very spacious, and contained all sorts of apartments, side rooms, round and square basins, small ovens, galleries, porticoes, etc., without counting a space for bodily exercises (*palœstra*) where the young Pompeians went through their gymnastics. This, it will be seen, was a complete water-cure establishment.

The most curious thing dug up out of these ruins is a Berosian sun-dial marked with an Oscan inscription announcing that N. Atinius, son of Marius the quæstor, had caused it to be executed, by order of the decurions, with the funds resulting from the public fines. Sun-dials were no rarity at Pompeii.

They existed there in every shape and of every price; among them was one elevated upon an Ionic column of *cipollino* marble. These primitive time-pieces were frequently offered by the Roman magistrates for the adornment of the monuments, a fact that greatly displeased a certain parasite whom Plautus describes:

"May the gods exterminate the man who first invented the hours!" he exclaims, "who first placed a sun-dial in this city! the traitor who has cut the day in pieces for my ill-luck! In my childhood there was no other time-piece than the stomach; and that is the best of them all, the most accurate in giving notice, unless, indeed, there be nothing to eat. But, nowadays, although the side-board be full, nothing is served up until it shall please the sun. Thus, since the town has become full of sun-dials, you see nearly everybody crawling about, half starved and emaciated."

The other thermæ of Pompeii are much smaller, but better adorned, and, above all, in better preservation. Would you like to take a full bath there in the antique style? You enter now by a small door in the rear, and traverse a corridor where five hundred lamps were found — a striking proof that the Pompeians passed at least a portion of the night at the baths. This corridor conducts you to the *apodyteres* or *spoliatorium*, the place where the bathers undress. At first blush you are rather startled at the idea of taking off your clothes in an apartment with six doors, but the ancients, who were better seasoned than we are, were not afraid of currents of air. While a slave takes your clothing and your sandals, and another, the *capsarius*, relieves you of your jewels, which he will deposit in a neighboring office, look at the apartment; the cornice ornamented with lyres and griffins, above which are ranges of lamps; the arched ceiling forming a semicircle divided off in white panels edged with red, and the white mosaic of the pavement bordered with black. Here are stone benches to sit down upon, and pins fixed in the walls, where the slave hangs up your white woollen toga and your tunic. Above there is a skylight formed of a single very thick pane of glass, and, firmly inclosed within an iron frame, which turns upon two pivots. The glass is roughened on one side to prevent inquisitive people from peeping into the hall where we are. On each side of the window some reliefs, now greatly damaged, represent combats of giants.

Here you are, as nude as an antique statue. Were you a true Roman, you would now step into an adjoining cabinet which was the anointing place (*elæthesium*), where the anointing with oil was done, and, after that, you will go and play tennis in the court, which was reached by a corridor now walled up. The blue vault was studded with golden stars. But you are not a true Roman; you have come hither simply to take a hot or a cold bath. If a cold one, pass on into the small room that opens at the end of the hall. It is the *frigidarium*.

This *frigidarium* or *natatio* is a circular room, which strikes you at the outset by its excellent state of preservation. In the middle of it is hollowed out a spacious round basin of white marble, four yards and a half in diameter by about four feet in depth; it might serve to-day—nothing is wanting but the water, says Overbeck. An inside circular series of steps enabled the Pompeians to bathe in a sitting posture. Four niches, prepared at the places where the angles would be if the apartment were square, contained benches where the bathers rested. The walls were painted yellow and adorned with green

11*

branches. The frieze and pediment were red and decorated with white bas-reliefs. The vault, which was blue and open overhead, was in the shape of a truncated cone. It was clear, brilliant, and gay, like the antique life itself.

Do you prefer a warm bath? Retrace your steps and, from the *apodyteros,* where you left your clothing, pass into the *tepidarium.* This hall, which is the richest of the bathing establishment, is paved in white mosaic with black borders, the vault richly ornamented with *stucature* and white paintings standing forth from a red and blue background. These reliefs in stucco represent cupids, chimeras, dolphins, does pursued by lions, etc. The red walls are adorned with closets, perhaps intended for the linen of the bathers, over which jutted a cornice supported by Atlases or Telamons in baked clay covered with stucco. A pretty border frame formed of arabesques separates the cornice from the vault. A large window at the extremity flanked by two figures in stucco lighted up the tepidarium, while subterranean conduits and a large brazier of bronze retained for it that lukewarm (*tepida*) temperature which gave it the peculiar name.

The Tepidarium, at the Baths.

This bronze brazier is still in existence, along with three benches of the same metal found in the same place; an inscription—*M. Nigidius Vaccula P. S.* (*pecuniâ sua*)—designates to us the donor who punning on his own name *Vaccula*, had caused a little cow to be carved upon the brazier; and on the feet of the benches, the hoofs of that quiet animal. The bottom of this precious heater formed a huge grating with bars of bronze, upon which bricks were laid; upon these bricks extended a layer of pumice-stones, and upon the pumice-stones the lighted coals.

What, then, was the use to which this handsome tepidarium was applied? Its uses were manifold, as you will learn farther on, but, for the moment, it is to prepare you, by a gentle warmth, for the temperature of the stove that you are going to enter through a door which closed of itself by its own weight, as the shape of the hinges indicates.

This caldarium is a long room at the ends of which rises, on one side, something like the parapet of a well, and on the other a square basin. The middle of the room is the stove, properly speaking.

The steam did not circulate in pipes, but exhaled from the wall itself and from the hollow ceiling in warm emanations. The adornments of the walls consisted of simple flutings. The square basin (*alveus* or *baptisterium*) which served for the warm baths was of marble. It was ascended by three steps and descended on the inside by an interior bench upon which ten bathers could sit together. Finally, on the other side of the room, in a semi-circular niche, rose the well parapet of which I spoke; it was a *labrum*, constructed with the public funds. An inscription informs us that it cost seven hundred and fifty sestertii, that is to say, something over thirty dollars. Yet this *labrum* is a large marble vessel seven feet in diameter. Marble has grown dearer since then.

On quitting the stove, or warm bath, the Pompeians wet their heads in that large wash-basin, where tepid water which must, at that moment, have seemed cold, leaped from a bronze pipe still visible. Others still more courageous plunged into the icy water of the frigidarium, and came out of it, they said, stronger and more supple in their limbs. I prefer believing them to imitating them.

Have you had enough of it? Would you leave the heating room? You belong to the slaves who are waiting for you, and will not let you go. You are streaming with perspiration, and the *tractator*, armed with a *strigilla*, or flesh brush, is there to rasp your body. You escape to the tepidarium; but it is there that the most cruel operations await you. You belong, as I remarked, to the slaves; one of them cuts your nails, another plucks out your stray hair, and a third still seeks to press your body and rasp the skin with his brush, a fourth prepares the most fearful frictions yet to ensue, while others deluge you with oils and essences, and grease you with perfumed unguents. You asked just now what was the use of the tepidarium; you now know, for you have been made acquainted with the Roman baths.

A word in reference to the unguents with which you have just been rubbed. They were of all kinds; you have seen the shops where they were sold. They were perfumed with myrrh, spikenard, and cinnamon; there was the Egyptian unguent for the feet and legs, the Phœnician for the cheeks and the breast, and the Sisymbrian for the two arms; the essence of marjorum for the eyebrows and the hair, and that of wild thyme for the nape of the neck and the keees. These unguents were very dear, but they kept up youth and health.

"How have you managed to preserve yourself so long and so well?" asked Augustus of Pollio.

"With wine inside, and oil outside," responded the old man.

As for the utensils of the baths (a collection of them is still preserved at the Naples museum on an iron ring), they consisted first of the strigilla, then of the little bottle or vial of oil, and a sort of stove called the *scaphium*. All these, along with the slippers, the apron, and the purse, composed the baggage that one took with him to the baths.

The most curious of these instruments was the strigilla or scraper, bent like a sickle and hollowed in a sort of channel. With this the slave *curried* the bather's body. The poor people of that country who bathed in the time of the Romans — they have not kept up the custom — and who had no strigillarii at their service, rubbed themselves against the wall.

One day the Emperor Hadrian seeing one of his veterans thus engaged, gave him money and slaves to strigillate him. A few days afterward, the Emperor, going to the baths, saw a throng of paupers who, whenever they caught sight of him, began to rub vigorously against the wall. He merely said: "Rub yourselves against each other!"

There were other apartments adjoining those that I have designated, and very similar to them, only simpler and not so well furnished. These modest baths served for the slaves, think some, and for the women, according to others. The latter opinion I think, lacks gallantry. In front of this edifice, at the principal entrance of the baths, opened a tennis-court, surrounded with columns and flanked by a crypt and a saloon. Many inscriptions covered the walls, among others the announcement of a show with a hunt, awnings, and sprinklings of perfumed water. It was there that the Pompeians assembled to hear the news concerning the public shows and the rumors of the day. There they could read the dispatches from Rome. This is no anachronism, good reader, for newspapers were known to the ancients — see Leclerc's book —

and they were called the *diurnes* or *daily doings* of
the Roman people; diurnals and journals are two
words belonging to the same family. Those ancient
newspapers were as good in their way as our own.
They told about actors who were hissed; about funeral ceremonies; of a rain of milk and blood that fell
during the consulate of M. Acilius and C. Porcius;
of a sea-serpent — but no, the sea-serpent is modern.
Odd facts like the following could be read in them.
This took place twenty eight years after Jesus Christ,
and must have come to the Pompeians assembled in
the baths: "When Titus Sabinus was condemned,
with his slaves, for having been the friend of Germ-
anicus, the dog of the former could not be got
away from the spot, but accompanied the prisoner to
the place of execution, uttering the most doleful howls
in the presence of a crowd of people. Some one
threw him a piece of bread and he carried it to his
master's lips, and when the corpse was tossed into the
Tiber, the dog dashed after it, and strove to keep it
on the surface, so that people came from all directions
to admire the animal's devotion."

We are nowhere informed that the Roman journals

were subjected to government stamp and security for good behavior, but they were no more free than those of France. Here is an anecdote reported by Dion on that subject:

"It is well known," he says, "that an artist restored a large portico at Rome which was threatening to fall, first by strengthening its foundations at all points, so that it could not be displaced. He then lined the walls with sheep's fleeces and thick mattresses, and, after having attached ropes to the entire edifice, he succeeded, by dint of manual force and the use of capstans, in giving it its former position. But Tiberius, through jealousy, would not allow the name of this artist to appear in the newspapers."

Now that you have been told a little concerning the ways of the Roman people, you may quit the Thermæ, but not without casting a glance at the heating apparatus visible in a small adjacent court. This you approach by a long corridor, from the *apodytera*. There you find the *hypocaust*, a spacious round fireplace which transmitted warm air through lower conduits to the stove, and heated the two boilers built into the masonry and supplied from a reservoir. From this reservoir the water fell cold into the first boiler, which sent it lukewarm into the second, and the latter, being closer to the fire, gave it forth at a boiling temperature. A conduit carried the hot water of the second boiler to the square basin of the calidarium and another conveyed the tepid water of the first boiler to the large receptacle of the labrum. In the fire-place was found a quantity of rosin which the Pompeians used in kindling their fires. Such were the Thermæ of a small Roman city.

VI.

THE DWELLINGS.

IN order, now, to study the *home* of antique times, we have but to cross the street of the baths obliquely. We thus reach the dwelling of the ædile Pansa. He, at least, is the proprietor designated by general opinion, which, according to my ideas, is wrong in this particular. An inscription painted on the door-post has given rise to this error. The inscription runs thus : *Pansam ædilem Paratus rogat.* This the early antiquarians translated : *Paratus invokes Pansa the ædile.* The early antiquaries erred. They should have rendered it : *Paratus demands Pansa for ædile.* It was not an invocation but an electoral nomination. We have already

(135)

deciphered many like inscriptions. Universal suf-
frage put itself forward among the ancients as it
does with us.

Hence, the dwelling that I am about to enter
was not that of Pansa, whose name is found thus
suggested for the ædileship in many other places,
but rather that of Paratus, who, in order to designate the candidate of his choice, wrote the name
on his door-post.

Such is my opinion, but, as one runs the risk of
muddling everything by changing names already
accepted, I do not insist upon it. So let us enter
the house of Pansa the ædile.

This dwelling is not the most ornate, but it is
the most regular in Pompeii, and also the least complicated and the most simply complete. Thus, all
the guides point it out as the model house, and perceiving that they are right in so doing, I will imi-
tate them.

In what did a Pompeian's dwelling differ from
a small stylish residence or villa of modern times?
In a thousand and one points which we shall discover, step by step, but chiefly in this, that it was

turned inwards, or, as it were, doubled upon itself; not that it was, as has been said, altogether a stranger to the street, and presented to the latter only a large painted wall, a sort of lofty screen. The upper stories of the Pompeian houses having nearly all crumbled, we are not in a position to affirm that they did not have windows opening on the public streets. I have already shown you *mœniana* or suspended balconies from which the pretty girls of the place could ogle the passers-by. But it is certain that the first floor, consisting of the finest and best occupied apartments, grouped its rooms around two interior courts and turned their backs to the street. Hence, these two courts opening one behind the other, the development of the front was but a small affair compared with the depth of the house.

These courts were called the *atrium* and the peristyle. One might say that the atrium was the public and the peristyle the private part of the establishment; that the former belonged to the world and the second to the family. This arrangement nearly corresponded with the division of the Greek

12*

dwelling into *andronitis* and *gynaikotis*, the side
for the men and the side for the women. Around
the atrium were usually ranged—we must not be
too rigorously precise in these distinctions — the
rooms intended for the people of the house, and
those who called upon them. Around the peristyle
were the rooms reserved for the private occupancy
of the family.

I commence with the atrium. It was reached
from the street by a narrow alley (the *prothyrum*),
opening, by a two-leaved door, upon the sidewalk.
The doors have been burned, but we can picture them
to ourselves according to the paintings, as being of
oak, with narrow panels adorned with gilded nails,
provided with a ring to open them by, and surmounted
with a small window lighting up the alley. They
opened inwards, and were secured by means of a bolt,
which shot vertically downward into the threshold
instead of reaching across.

I enter right foot foremost, according to the Roman
custom (to enter with the left foot was a bad omen);
and I first salute the inscription on the threshold
(*salve*) which bids me welcome. The porter's lodge

The Atrium in the House of Pansa, restored.

(*cella ostiarii*) was usually hollowed out in the entry-way, and the slave in question was sometimes chained, a precaution which held him at his post, undoubtedly, but which hindered him from pursuing robbers. Sometimes, there was only a dog on guard, in his place, or merely the representation of a dog in mosaic : there is one in excellent preservation at the Museum in Naples retaining the famous inscription (*Cave canem*) — "Beware of the dog! "

The atrium was not altogether a court, but rather a large hall covered with a roof, in the middle of which opened a large bay window. Thus the air and the light spread freely throughout the spacious room, and the rain fell from the sky or dripped down over the four sloping roofs into a marble basin, called *impluvium*, that conveyed it to the cistern, the mouth of which is still visible. The roofs usually rested on large cross-beams fixed in the walls. In such case, the atrium was Tuscan, in the old fashion. Some-times, the roofs rested on columns planted at the four corners of the impluvium: then, the opening en-larged, and the atrium became a tetrastyle. Some authors mention still other kinds of *atria* — the Co·

rinthian, which was richly decorated; the *dipluviatum*, where the roof, instead of sloping inward, sloped outward and threw off the rain-water into the street; the *testudinatum*, in which the roof looked like an immense tortoise-shell, etc. But these forms of roofs, especially the last mentioned, were rare, and the Tuscan atrium was almost everywhere predominant, as we find it on Pansa's house.

Place yourself at the end of the alley, with your back toward the street, and you command a view of this little court and its dependencies. It is needless to say that the roof has disappeared: the eruption consumed the beams, the tiles have been broken by falling, and not only the tiles but the antefixes, cut in palm-leaves or in lion's heads, which spouted the water into the impluvium. Nothing remains but the basin and the partition walls which marked the subdivisions of the ground-floor. One first discovers a room of considerable size at the end, between a smaller room and a corridor, and eight other side cabinets. Of these eight cabinets, the six that come first, three to the right and three to the left, were bedrooms, or *cubicula*. What first strikes the observer is their diminutive size. There was room only for the bed, which was frequently indicated by an elevation of the masonry, and on that mattresses or sheepskins were stretched. The bedsteads often were also of bronze or wood, quite like those or our time. These cubicula received the air and the light through the door, which the Pompeians probably left open in summer.

Next to the cubicula came laterally the *alae,* the wings, in which Pansa (if not Paratus) received his visitors in the morning — friends, clients, parasites. These rooms must have been rich, paved, as they were, with lozenges of marble and surrounded with seats or divans. The large room at the end was the *tablinum*, which separated, or rather connected, the two courts and ascended by two steps to the peristyle. In this tablinum, which was a show-room or parlor, were kept the archives of the family, and the *imagines majorum*, or images of ancestors, which were wax figures extolled in grand inscriptions, stood there in rows. You have observed that they were conducted with great pomp in the funeral processions. The Romans did not despise these exhibitions of vanity. They clung all the more tenaciously to their ancestry as they became more and more separated from them by the lapse of ages and the decay of old manners and customs.

To the left of the tablinum opened the library, where were found some volumes, unfortunately almost destroyed; and off to the right of the tablinum ran the fauces, a narrow corridor leading to the peristyle.

Thus, a show-room, two reception rooms, a library, six bedchambers for slaves or for guests, and all these ranged around a hall lighted from above, paved in white mosaic with black edging between and adorned with a marble basin, — such is the atrium of Pansa.

I am now going to pass beyond into the fauces. An apartment opens upon this corridor and serves as a pendant to the library; it is a bedroom, as a recess left in the thickness of the wall for the bedstead indicates. A step more and I reach the peristyle.

The peristyle is a real court or a garden surrounded with columns forming a portico. In the house of Pansa, the sixteen columns, although originally Doric, had been repaired in the Corinthian style by means of a replastering of stucco. In some houses they were connected by balustrades or walls breast high, on which flowers in either vases or boxes of marble were placed, and in one Pompeian house there was a frame set with glass panes. In the midst of the court was hollowed out a spacious basin (*piscina*), sometimes replaced by a parterre from which the water leaped gaily. In the peristyle of Pansa's house is still seen, in an intercolumniation, the mouth of a cistern. We are now in the richest and most favored part of the establishment.

At the end opens the *œcus*, the most spacious hall, surrounded, in the houses of the opulent Romans, with columns and galleries, decorated with precious marbles developing into a basilica. But in the house of Pansa do not look for such splendors. Its œcus was but a large chamber between the peristyle and a garden.

To the right of the œcus, at the end of the court, is half hidden a smaller and less obtrusive apartment, probably an *exedra*. On the right wing of the peristyle, on the last range, recedes the triclinium. The word signifies triple bed; three beds

in fine, ranged in horse-shoe order, occupied this
apartment, which served as a dining-room. It is
well known that the ancients took their meals in
a reclining attitude and resting on their elbows.
This Carthaginian custom, imported by the Punic
wars, had become established everywhere, even at
Pompeii. The ancients said "make the beds," instead of " lay the table."

To the right of the peristyle on the first range,
glides a corridor receding toward a private door
that opens on a small side street. This was the
posticum, by which the master of the house evaded
the importunate visitors who filled the atrium.
This method of escaping bores was called *postico
fallere clientem.* It was a device that must have
been familiar to rich persons who were beset
every morning by a throng of petitioners and
hangers-on.

The left side of the peristyle was occupied by
three bedchambers, and by the kitchen, which was
hidden at the end, to the left of the œcus. This
kitchen, like most of the others, has its fireplaces
and ovens still standing. They contained ashes and

even coal when they were discovered, not to mention the cooking utensils in terra cotta and in bronze. Upon the walls were painted two enormous serpents, sacred reptiles which protected the altar of Fornax, the culinary divinity. Other paintings (a hare, a pig, a wild boar's head, fish, etc.) ornamented this room adjoining which was, in the olden time among the Pompeians, as to-day among the Neapolitans, the most ignoble retreat in the dwelling. A cabinet close by served for a pantry, and there were found in it a large table and jars of oil ranged along on a bench.

Thus a large portico with columns, surrounding a court adorned with a marble basin (*piscina*); around the portico on the right, three bed-chambers or *cubicula;* on the right, a rear door (*posticum*) and an eating room (*triclinium*); at the end, the grand saloon (*œcus*), between an exedra and kitchen — such was the peristyle of Pansa.

This relatively spacious habitation had still a third depth (allow me the expression) behind the peristyle. This was the *xysta* or garden, divided off posed small rooms altogether independent of the house, and probably occupied by *inquilini*,* or lodgers, a class of people despised among the ancients, who highly esteemed the homestead idea. A Roman who did not live under his own roof would cut as poor a figure as a Parisian who did not occupy his own furnished rooms, or a Neapolitan compelled to go afoot. Hence, the petty townsmen clubbed together to build or buy a house, which they owned in common, preferring the inconveniences of a divided proprietorship to those of a mere temporary occupancy. But they have greatly changed their notions in that country, for now they move every year.

I have done no more here than merely to sketch the plan of the house. Would you refurnish it? Then, rifle the Naples museum, which has despoiled it. You will find enough of bedsteads, in the collection of bronzes there, for the cubicula; enough of carved benches, tables, stands, and precious vases for the œcus, the exedra, and the wings, and enough of lamps to hang

---

* So strong was this feeling, that the very name *inquilinus*, or lodger, was an insult. Cicero not having been born at Rome, Catiline called him offensively *civis inquilinus* — a lodger citizen. (*Sallust.*)

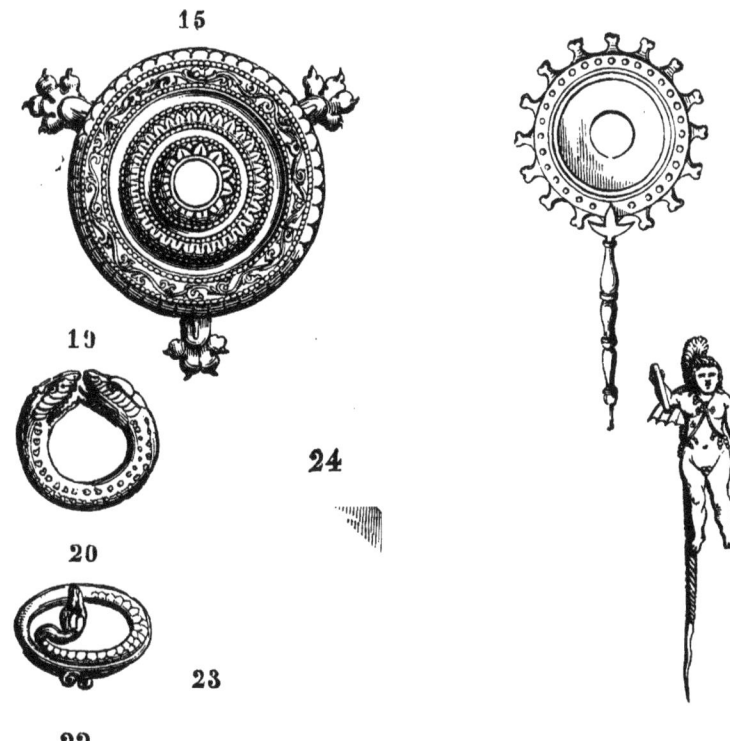

15

19

24

20

23

22

28

Candelabra, Jewelry, and Kitch

up; enough of candelabra to place in the saloons. Stretch carpets over the costly mosaic pavements and even over the simple *opus signinum* (a mixture of lime and crushed brick) which covered the floor of the unpretending chambers with a solid incrustation. Above all, replace the ceilings and the roofs, and then the doors and draperies; in fine, revive upon all these walls — the humblest as well as the most splendid — the bright and vivid pictures now effaced. What light, and what a gay impression! How all these clear, bold colors gleam out in the sunshine, which descends in floods from an open sky into the peristyle and the atrium! But that is not all: you must conjure up the dead. Arise, then, and obey our call, O young Pompeians of the first century! I summon Pansa, Paratus, their wives, their children, their slaves; the ostiarius, who kept the door; the *atriensis*, who controlled the atrium; the *scoparius*, armed with his birch-broom; the *cubicularii*, who were the bedroom servants; the *pedagogue*, my colleague, who was a slave like the rest, although he was absolute master of the library, where he alone, perhaps, understood the secrets of

13*

the papyri it contained. I hasten to the kitchen:
I want to see it as it was in the ancient day, — the
carnarium, provided with pegs and nails for the
fresh provisions, is suspended to the ceiling; the cooking ranges are garnished with chased stew-pans and
coppers, and large bronze pails, with luxurious handles,
are ranged along on the floor; the walls are covered
with shining utensils, long-handled spoons bent in
the shape of a swan's neck and head, skillets and
frying-pans, the spit and its iron stand, gridirons,
pastry-moulds (patty-pans?) fish-moulds (*formella*),
and what is no less curious, the *apalare* and the *trua*,
flat spoons pierced with holes either to fry eggs or
to beat up liquids, and, in fine, the funnels, the sieves,
the strainers, the *colum vinarium*, which they
covered with snow and then poured their wine over
it, so that the latter dropped freshened and cooled
into the cups below, — all rare and precious relics
preserved by Vesuvius, and showing in what odd
corners elegance nestled, as Moliere would have said,
among the Romans of the olden times.

None but men entered this kitchen: they were the
cook, or *coquus*, and his subaltern, the slave of the

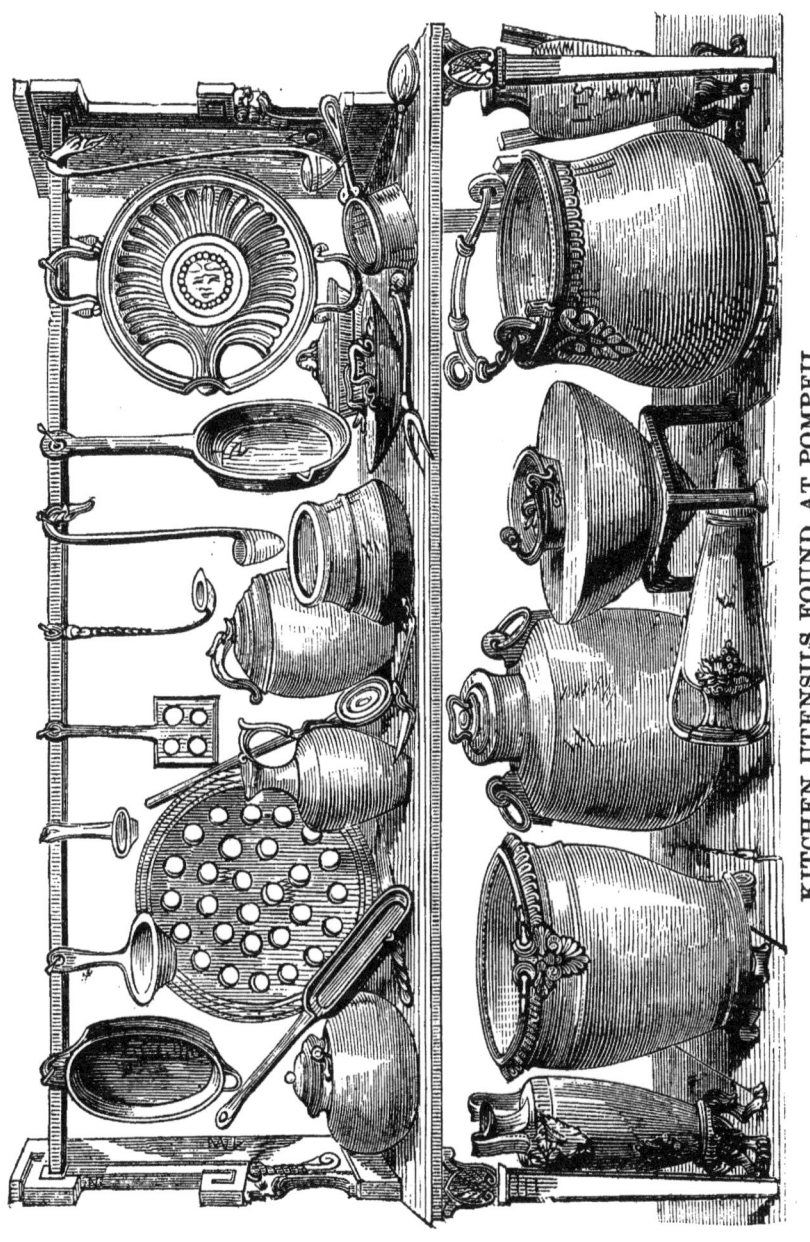

KITCHEN UTENSILS FOUND AT POMPEII.

slave, *focarius*. The meal is ready, and now come other slaves assigned to the table,— the *tricliniarches*, or foreman of all the rest; the *lectisterniator*, who makes the beds; the *praegustator*, who tastes the viands beforehand to reassure his master; the *structor*, who arranges the dishes on the plateaux or trays; the *scissor*, who carves the meats; and the young *pocillatro*, or *pincerna*, who pours out the wine into the cups, sometimes dancing as he does so (as represented by Moliere) with the airs and graces of a woman or a spoiled child.

There is festivity to-day: Paratus sups with Pansa, or rather Pansa with Paratus, for I persist in thinking that we are in the house of the elector and not of the future ædile. If the master of the house be a real Roman like Cicero, he rose early this morning and began the day with receiving visits. He is rich, and therefore has many friends, and has them of three kinds,— the *salutatores*, the *ductores*, and the *assectatores*. The first-named call upon him at his own house; the second accompany him to public meetings; and the third never leave him at all in public. He has, besides, a number of clients, whom he protects and whom he calls "my father" if they be

old, and "my brother" if they be young. There are
others who come humbly to offer him a little basket
(*sportula*), which they carry away full of money or
provisions. This morning Paratus has sent off his visitors expeditiously ; then, as he is no doubt a pious
man, he has gone through his devotions before the
domestic altar, where his household gods are ranged.
We know that he offered peculiar worship to Bacchus,
for he had a little bronze statue of that god, with silver
eyes; it was, I think, at the entrance of his garden,
in a kettle, wrapped up with other precious articles,
Paratus tried to save this treasure on the day of the
eruption, but he had to abandon it in order to save
himself. But to continue my narration of the day as
this Pompeian spent it. His devotions over, he took a
turn to the Forum, the Exchange, the Basilica, where
he supported the candidature of Pansa. From there,
unquestionably, he did not omit going to the Thermæ,
a measure of health ; and, now, at length, he has just
returned to his home. During his absence, his slaves
have cleansed the marbles, washed the stucco, covered
the pavements with sawdust, and, if it be in winter,
have lit fuel on large bronze braziers in the open air and

borne them into the saloons, for there are no chimneys anywhere. The expected guest at length arrives — salutations to Pansa, the future ædile! Meanwhile Sabina, the wife of Paratus, has not remained inactive. She has passed the whole morning at her toilet, for the toilet of a Sabina, Pompeian or Roman, is an affair of state, — see Boettger's book. As she awoke she snapped her fingers to summon her slaves, and the poor girls have hastened to accomplish this prodigious piece of work. First, the applier of cosmetics has effaced the wrinkles from the brows of her mistress, and, then, with her saliva, has prepared her rouge; then, with a needle, she has painted her mistress' eyelashes and eyebrows, forming two well-arched and tufted lines of jetty hue, which unite at the root of the nose. This operation completed, she has washed Sabina's teeth with rosin from Scio, or more simply, with pulverized pumice-stone, and, finally, has overspread her entire countenance with the white powder of lead which was much used by the Romans at that early day.

Then came the *ornatrix*, or hairdresser. The fair Romans dyed their hair blonde, and when the dyeing process was not sufficient, they wore wigs. This example was followed by the artists, who put wigs on their statues; in France they would put on crinoline. Ancient head-dresses were formidable monuments held up with pins of seven or eight inches in length. One of these pins, found at Herculaneum, is surmounted with a Corinthian capital upon which a carved Venus is twisting her hair with both hands while she looks into a mirror that Cupid holds up before her. The mirrors of those ancient days — let us exhaust the subject! — were of polished metal; the richest were composed of a plate of silver applied upon a plate of gold and sustained by a carved handle of wood or ivory; and Seneca exclaimed, in his testy indignation, "The dowry that the Senate once bestowed upon the daughter of Scipio would no longer suffice to pay for the mirror of a freedwoman!"

At length, Sabina's hair is dressed: Heaven grant that she may be pleased with it, and may not, in a fit of rage, plunge one of her long pins into the naked shoulder of the ornatrix! Now comes the slave who cuts her nails, for never would a Roman lady, or a Roman gentleman either, who had any self-respect, have deigned to perform this operation with their own

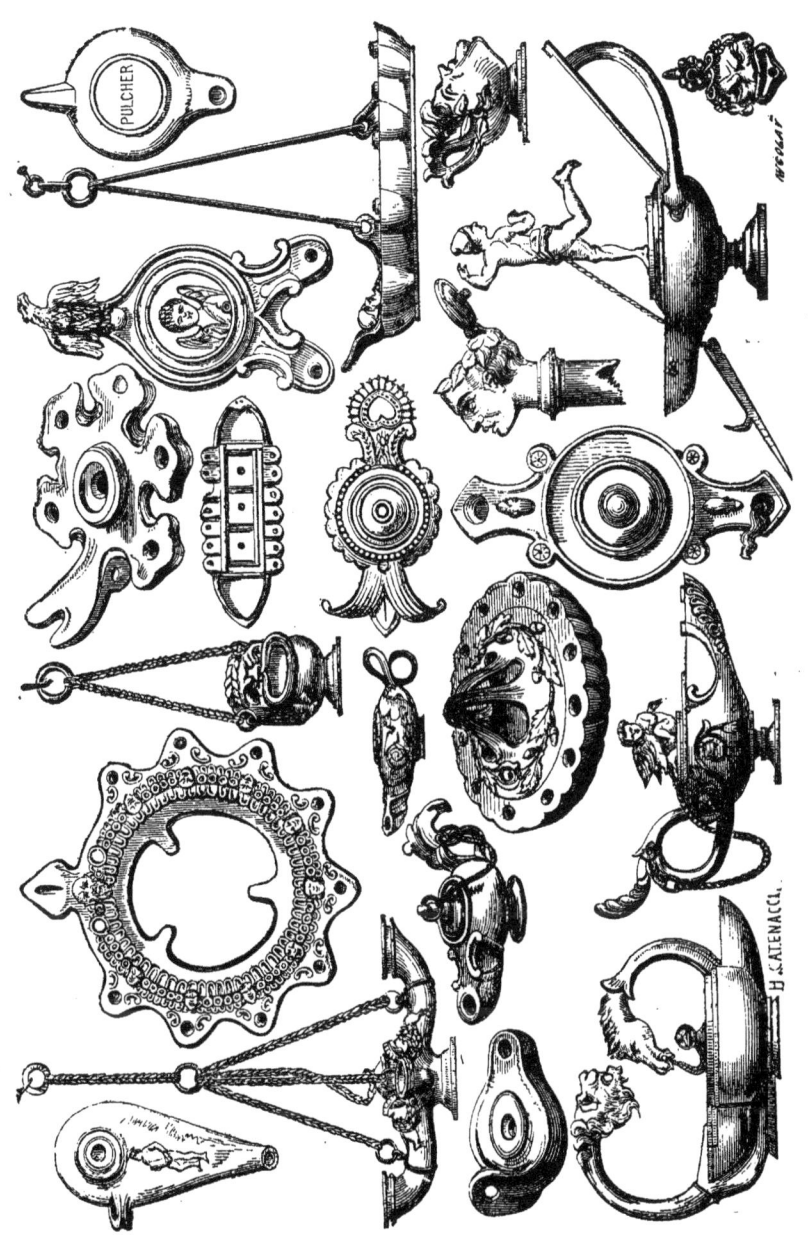

Lamps of Earthenware and Bronze found at Pompeii.

hands. It was to the barber or *tonsor* that this office was assigned, along with the whole masculine toilet, generally speaking; that worthy shaved you, clipped you, plucked you, even washed you and rubbed your skin; perfumed you with unguents, and curried you with the strigilla if the slaves at the bath had not already done so. Horace makes great sport of an eccentric who used to pare his own nails.

Sabina then abandons her hands to a slave who, armed with a set of small pincers and a penknife (the ancients were unacquainted with scissors), acquitted themselves skilfully of that delicate task — a most grave affair and a tedious operation, as the Roman ladies wore no gloves. Gesticulation was for them a science learnedly termed *chironomy*. Like a skilful instrument, pantomime harmoniously accompanied the voice. Hence, all those striking expressions that we find in authors, — "the subtle devices of the fingers," as Cicero has it; the "loquacious hand" of Petronius. Recall to your memory the beautiful hands of Diana and Minerva, and these two lines of Ovid, which naturally come in here:

"Exiguo signet gestu quodcunque loquetur,
Cui digiti pingues, cui scaber unguis erit." *

The nail-paring over, there remains the dressing
of the person, to be accomplished by other slaves. Tho
seamstresses (*carcinatrices*) belonged to the least-
important class ; for that matter, there was little or no
sewing to do on the garments of the ancients.
Lucretia had been dead for many years, and the
matrons of the empire did not waste their time in
spinning wool. When Livia wanted to make the
garments of Augustus with her own hands, this
fancy of the Empress was considered to be in very
bad taste. A long retinue of slaves (cutters, linen-
dressers, folders, etc.), shared in the work of the
feminine toilet, which, after all, was the simplest that
had been worn since the nudity of the earliest days.
Over the scarf which they called *trophium*, and which
sufficed to hold up their bosoms, the Roman ladies
passed a long-sleeved *subucula*, made of fine wool, and
over that they wore nothing but the tunic when in the
house. The *libertinæ*, or simple citizens' wives and

* Let not fingers that are too thick, and ill-pared nails, make
gestures too conspicuous.

daughters, wore this robe short and coming scarcely to the knee, so as to leave in sight the rich bracelets that they wore around their legs. But the matrons lengthened the ordinary tunic by means of a plaited furbelow or flounce (*instita*), edged, sometimes, with golden or purple thread. In such case, it took the name of *stola*, and descended to their feet. They knotted it at the waist, by means of a girdle artistically hidden under a fold of the tucked-up garment. Below the tunic, the women when on the street wore, lastly, their *toga*, which was a roomy mantle enveloping the bosom and flung back over the left shoulder; and thus attired, they moved along proudly, draped in white woollens.

At length, the wife of Paratus is completely attired; she has drawn on the white bootees worn by matrons; unless, indeed, she happens to prefer the sandals worn by the libertinæ,— the freedwomen were so called, — which left those large, handsome Roman feet, which we should like to see a little smaller, uncovered. The selection of her jewelry is now all that remains to be done. Sabina owned some curious specimens that were found in the ruins of her house. The Latins had a discourteous word to designate this collection of precious knick-knackery; they called it the "woman's world," as though it were indeed all that there was in the world for women. One room in the Museum at Naples is full of these exhumed trinkets, consisting of serpents bent into rings and bracelets, circlets of gold set with carved stones, ear-rings representing sets of scales, clusters of pearls, threads of gold skilfully twisted into necklaces; chaplets to which hung amulets, of more or less decent design, intended as charms to ward off ill-luck; pins with carved heads; rich clasps that held up the tunic sleeves or the gathered folds of the mantle, cameoed with a superb relief and of exquisite workmanship worthy of Greece; in fine, all that luxury and art, sustaining each other, could invent that was most wonderful. The Pompeian ladies, in their character of provincials, must have carried this love of baubles that cost them so dearly, to extremes: thus, they wore them in their hair, in their ears, on their necks, on their shoulders, their arms, their wrists, their legs, even on their ankles and their feet, but especially on their hands, every finger of which, excepting the middle one, was covered with rings up to the third joint,

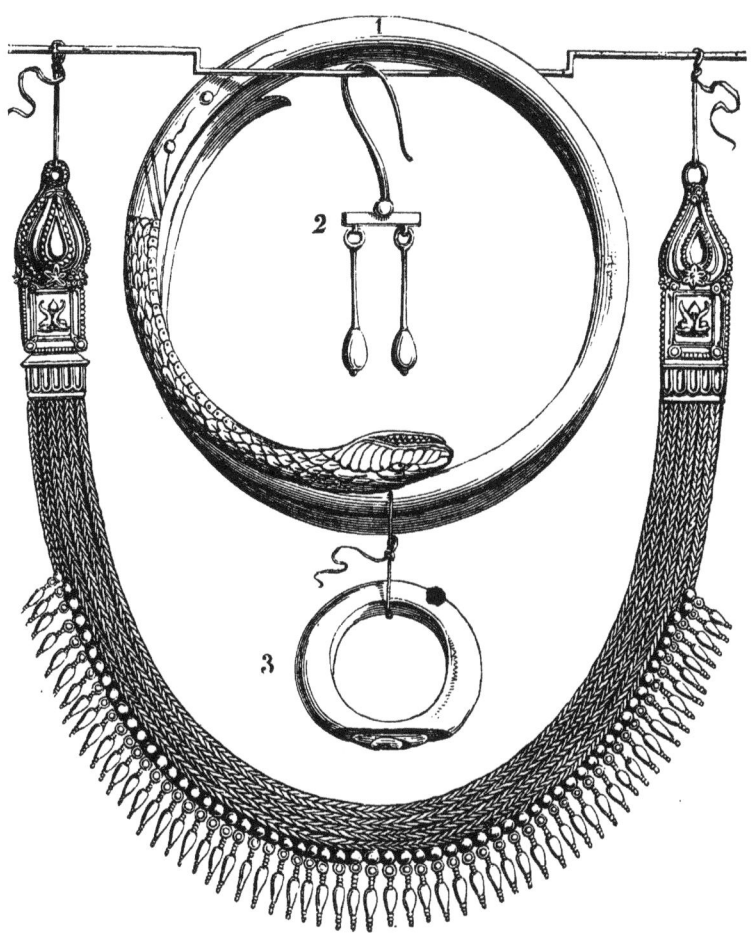

Necklace, Ring, Bracelets, and Ear-rings found at Pompeii.

where their lovers slipped on those that they desired to exchange with them.

Her toilet completed, Sabina descended from her room in the upper story. The ordinary guests, the friend of the house, the clients and *the shadows* (such was the name applied to the supernumeraries, the humble doubles whom the invited guests brought with them), awaited her in the peristyle. Nine guests in all — the number of the Muses. It was forbidden to exceed that total at the suppers of the triclinium. There were never more than nine, nor less than three, the number of the Graces. When a great lord invited six thousand Romans to his table, the couches were laid in the atrium. But there is not an atrium in Pompeii that could contain the hundredth part of that number.

The ninth hour of the day, i. e., the third or fourth in the afternoon, has sounded, and it is now that the supper begins in all respectable houses. Some light collations, in the morning and at noon, have only sharpened the appetites of the guests. All are now assembled; they wash their hands and their feet, leave their sandals at the door, and are shown into the triclinium.

The three bronze bedsteads are covered with cushions and drapery; the one at the end (*the medius*) in one corner´ represents the place of honor reserved for the important guest, the consular personage. On the couch to the right recline the host, the hostess, and the friend of the house. The other guests take the remaining places. Then, in come the slaves bearing trays, which they put, one by one, upon the small bronze table with the marble top which is stationed between the three couches like a tripod. Ah! what glowing descriptions I should have to make were I at the house of Trimalcion or Lucullus! I should depict to you the winged hares, the pullets and fish carved in pieces, with pork meat; the wild boar served up whole upon an enormous platter and stuffed with living thrushes, which fly out in every direction when the boar's stomach is cut open; the side dishes of birds' tongues; of enormous *murenæ* or eels; barbel caught in the Western Ocean and stifled in salt pickle; surprises of all kinds for the guests, such as sets of dishes descending from the ceiling, fantastic apparitions, dancing girls, mountebanks, gladiators, trained female athletes,—all the orgies, in fine, of those strange old times. But let us not forget where we really are. Paratus is not an emperor, and has to confine himself to a simple citizen repast, quiet and unassuming throughout. The bill of fare of one of these suppers has been preserved, and here we give it

First Course.—Sea urchins. Raw oysters at discretion. *Pelorides* or palourdes (a sort of shell-fish now found on the coasts of Poitou in France). Thorny shelled oysters; larks; a hen pullet with asparagus; stewed oysters and mussels; white and black sea-tulips.

Second Course.—*Spondulae*, a variety of oyster; sweet water mussels; sea nettles; becaficoes; cutlets of kid and boar's meat; chicken pie; becaficoes again, but differently prepared, with an asparagus sauce; *murex* and purple fish. The latter were but different kinds of shell-fish.

Third Course.—The teats of a sow *au naturel;* they were cut as soon as the animal had littered; wild boar's head (this was the main dish); sow's teats in a ragout; the breasts and necks of roast ducks; fricasseed wild duck; roast. hare, a great delicacy; roasted Phrygian chickens; starch cream; cakes from Vicenza.

All this was washed down with the light Pompeian wine, which was not bad, and could be kept for ten years, if boiled. The wine of Vesuvius, once highly esteemed, has lost its reputation, owing to the concoctions now sold to travellers under the label of *Lachrymæ Christi*. The vintages of the volcano must have been more honestly prepared at the period when they were sung by Martial. Every day there is found in the cellars of Pompeii some short-necked, full-bodied, and elongated *amphora*, terminating in a point so as to stick upright in the ground, and nearly all are marked with an inscription stating the age and origin of the liquor they contained. The names of the consuls usually designated the year of the vintage. The further back the consul, the more respectable the wine. A Roman, in the days of the Empire, having been asked under what consul his wine dated, boldly replied, "Under none!"

thereby proclaiming that his cellar had been stocked under the earliest kings of Rome.

These inscriptions on the amphoræ make us acquainted with an old Vesuvian wine called *picatum*, or, in other words, with a taste of pitch; *fundanum*, or Fondi wine, much esteemed, and many others. In fine, let us not forget the famous growth of Falernus, sung by the poets, which did not disappear until the time of Theodoric.

But besides the amphoræ, how much other testimony there still remains of the olden libations,— those rich *crateræ*, or broad, shallow goblets of bronze damascened with silver; those delicately chiselled cups; those glasses and bottles which Vesuvius has preserved for us; that jug, the handle of which is formed of a satyr bending backward to rub his shoulders against the edge of the vase; those vessels of all shapes on which eagles perch or swans and serpents writhe; those cups of baked clay adorned with so many arabesques and inviting descriptions. " Friend," says one of them " drink of my contents."

"Friend of my soul, this goblet sip !"

rhymes the modern bard.

What a mass of curious and costly things! What is the use of rummaging in books! With the museums of Naples before us, we can reconstruct all the triclinia of Pompeii at a glance.

There, then, are the guests, gay, serene, reclining or leaning on their elbows on the three couches. The table is before them, but only to be looked at, for slaves are continually moving to and fro, from one to the other, serving every guest with a portion of each dish on a slice of bread. Pansa daintily carries the delicate morsel offered him to his mouth with his fingers, and flings the bread under the table, where a slave, in crouching attitude, gathers up all the debris of the repast. No forks are used, for the ancients were unacquainted with them. At the most, they knew the use of the spoon or cochlea, which they employed in eating eggs. After each dish they dipped their fingers in a basin presented to them, and then wiped them upon a napkin that they carried with them as we take our handkerchiefs with us. The wealthiest people had some that were very costly and which they threw into the fire when they had been soiled; the fire cleansed without burning them. Refined people wiped their fingers on the hair of the cupbearers, — another Oriental usage. Recollect Jesus and Mary Magdalene.

At length, the repast being concluded, the guests took off their wreaths, which they stripped of their leaves into a goblet that was passed around the circle for every one to taste, and this ceremony concluded the libations.

I have endeavored to describe the supper of a rich Pompeian and exhibit his dwelling as it would appear reconstructed and re-occupied. Reduce its dimensions and simplify it as much as possible by suppressing the peristyle, the columns, the paintings, the tablinum, the exedra, and all the rooms devoted to pleasure or vanity, and you will have the house of a poor man. On the contrary, if you develop it, by enriching it beyond measure, you may build in your fancy one of those superb Roman palaces, the extravagant luxuriousness of which augmented, from day to day, under the emperors. Lucius Crassus, who was the first to introduce columns of foreign marble, in his dwelling, erected only six of them but twelve feet high. At a later period, Marcus Scaurus surrounded his atrium with a colonnade of black marble rising thirty-eight feet above the soil. Mamurra did not stop at so fair a limit. That distinguished Roman knight covered his whole house with marble. The residence of Lepidus was the handsomest in Rome seventy-eight years before Christ. Thirty-five years later, it was but the hundredth. In spite of some attempts at reaction by Augustus, this passion for splendor reached a frantic pitch. A freedman in the reign of Claudius decorated his triclinium with thirty-two columns of onyx. I say nothing of the slaves that were counted by thousands in the old palaces, and by hundreds in the triclinium and kitchen alone.

"O ye beneficent gods! how many men employed to serve a single stomach!" exclaimed Seneca, who passed in his day for a master of rhetoric. In our time, he would be deemed a socialist.

Peristyle of the House of the Quaestor at Pompeii.

VII.

ART IN POMPEII.

The house of Pansa was large, but not much ornamented. There are others which are shown in preference to the visitor. Let us mention them concisely in the catalogue and inventory style:

The house of the Faun. — Fine mosaics; a masterpiece in bronze; the Dancing Faun, of which we shall speak farther on. Besides the atrium and the peristyle, a third court, the xysta, surrounded with forty-four columns, duplicated on the upper story. Numberless precious things were found there, in the presence of the son of Goethe. The owner was a wine-merchant. (?)

The house of the Quæstor, or of Castor and Pollux.

— Large safes of very thick and very hard wood, lined with copper and ornamented with arabesques, perhaps the public money-chests, hence this was probably the residence of the quæstor who had charge of the public funds; a Corinthian atrium; fine paintings —the *Bacchante*, the *Medea*, the *Children of Niobe*, etc. Rich development of the courtyards.

The house of the Poet. — Homeric paintings; celebrated mosaics; the dog at the doorsill, with the inscription *Cave Canem*; the *Choragus causing the recitation of a piece.* All these are at the museum.

The house of Sallust. — A fine bronze group; Hercules pursuing a deer (taken to the Museum at Palermo); a pretty stucco relievo in one of the bedchambers; Three couches of masonry in the triclinium; a decent and modest *venereum* that ladies may visit. There is seen an Acteon surprising Diana in the bath, the stag's antlers growing on his forehead and the hounds tearing him. The two scenes connect in the same picture, as in the paintings of the middle ages. Was this a warning to rash people? This venereum contained a bedchamber, a triclinium and a lararium, or small marble niche in which the household god was enshrined

Peristyle of the House of the Quæstor at Pompeii.

The house of Marcus Lucretius.—Very curious. A peristyle forming a sort of platform, occupied with baubles, which they have had the good taste to leave there; a miniature fountain, little tiers of seats, a small conduit, a small fish-tank, grotesque little figures in bronze, statuettes and images of all sorts,— Bacchus and Bacchantes, Fauns and Satyrs, one of which, with its arm raised above its head, is charming. Another in the form of a Hermes holds a kid in its arms; the she-goat trying to get a glimpse of her little one, is raising her fore-feet as though to clamber up on the spoiler. These odds and ends make up a pretty collection of toys, a shelf, as it were, on an ancient what-not of knick-knacks.

Then, there are the Adonis and the Hermaphrodite in the house of Adonis; the sacrarium or domestic chapel in the house of the Mosaic Columns; the wild beasts adorning the house of the Hunt; above all, the fresh excavations, where the paintings retain their undiminished brilliance. But if all these houses are to be visited, they are not to be described. Antiquaries dart upon this prey with frenzy, measuring the tiniest stone, discussing the

15

smallest painting, and leaving not a single frieze
or panel without some comment, so that, after
having read their remarks, one fancies that everything is precious in this exhumed curiosity-shop.
These folks deceive themselves and they deceive
us; their feelings as virtuosos thoroughly exhaust
themselves upon a theme which is very attractive,
very curious, 'tis true, but which calls for less completely scientific hands to set it to music, the more
so .that in Pompeii there is nothing grand, or
massive, or difficult to comprehend. Everything
stands right forth to the gaze and explains itself
as clearly and sharply as the light of day.

Moreover, these houses have been despoiled.
I might tell you of a pretty picture or a rich mosaic
in such-and-such a room. You would go thither
to look for it and not find it. The museum at
Naples has it, and if it be not there it is nowhere.
Time, the atmosphere, and the sunlight have destroyed it. Therefore, those who make out an
inventory of these houses for you are preparing
you bitter disappointments.

The only way to get an idea of Pompeian art

is not to examine all these monuments separately, but to group them in one's mind, and then to pay the museum an attentive visit. Thus we can put together a little ideal city, an artistic Pompeii, which we are going to make the attempt to explore.

Pompeii had two and even three forums. The third was a market; the first, with which you are already acquainted, was a public square; the other, which we are about to visit, is a sort of Acropolis, inclosed like that of Athens, and placed upon the highest spot of ground in the city. From a bench, still in its proper position at the extremity of this forum, you may distinguish the valley of the Sarno, the shady mountains that close its perspective, the cultivated checker-work of the country side, green tufts of the woodlands, and then the gently curving coast-line where Stabiæ wound in and out, with the picturesque heights of Sorrento, the deep blue of the sea, the transparent azure of the heavens, the infinite limpidity of the distant horizon, the brilliant clearness and the antique color. Those who have not beheld this scenery, can only half comprehend its monuments, which would ever be out of place beneath another sky.

It was in this bright sunlight that the Pompeian Acropolis, the triangular Forum, stood. Eight Ionic columns adorned its entrance and sustained a portico of the purest elegance, from which ran two long slender colonnades widening apart from each other and forming an acute angle. They are still surmounted with their architrave, which they lightly supported. The terrace, looking out upon the country and the sea, formed the third side of the triangle, in the middle of which rose some altars, — the ustrinum, in which the dead were burned, a small round temple covering a sacred well, and, finally, a Greek temple rising above all the rest from the height of its foundation and marking its columns unobstructedly against the sky. This platform, resting upon solid supports and covered with monuments in a fine style of art, was the best written page and the most substantially correct one in Pompeii. Unfortunately, here, as everywhere else, stucco had been plastered over the stone-work. The columns were painted. Nowhere could a front of pure marble—the white on the blue—be seen defined against the sky.

The remaining temples furnish us few data on architecture. You know those of the Forum. The temple of Fortune, now greatly dilapidated, must have resembled that of Jupiter. Erected by Marcus Tullius, a reputed relative of Cicero, it yields us nothing but very mediocre statues and inscriptions full of errors, proving that the priesthood of the place, by no means Ciceronian in their acquirements, did not thoroughly know even their own language. The temple of Esculapius, besides its altar, has retained a very odd capital, Corinthian if you will, but on which cabbage leaves, instead of the acanthus, are seen enveloping a head of Neptune. The temple of Isis, still standing, is more curious than handsome. It shows * that the Egyptian goddess was venerated at Pompeii, but it tells us nothing about antique art. It is entered at the side, by a sort of corridor leading into the sacred inclosure. The temple is on the right; the columns inclose it; a vaulted niche is hollowed out beneath the altar, where it served as a hiding-place for the priests, —at least so say the romance-writers. Un-

[* See note on page 198.]

15*

fortunately for this idea, the doorway of the recess stood forth and still stands forth to the gaze, rendering the alleged trickery impossible.

Behind the cella, another niche contained a statue of Bacchus, who was, perhaps, the same god as Osiris. An expurgation room, intended for ablutions and purifications, descending to a subterranean reservoir, occupied an angle of the courtyard. In front of this apartment stands an altar, on which were found some remnants of sacrifices. Isis, then, was the only divinity invoked at the moment of the eruption. Her painted statue held a cross with a handle to it, in one hand, and a cithera in the other, and her hair fell in long and carefully curled ringlets.

This is all that the temples give us. Artistically speaking, it is but little. Neither are the other monuments much richer in their information concerning ancient architecture. They let us know that the material chiefly employed consisted of lava, of tufa, of brick, excellently prepared, having more surface and less thickness than ours; of *peperino* (Sarno stone), which time renders very hard, sometimes with travertine and even marble in the ornaments; then there was Roman mortar, celebrated for its solidity, less perfect at Pompeii, however, than at Rome ; and finally, the stucco surface, covering the entire city with its smooth and polished crust, like a variegated mantle. But these edifices tell us nothing in particular; there is neither a style peculiar to Pompeii discernible in them, nor do we find artists of the place bearing any noted name, or possessing any singularity of taste and method. On the other hand, there is an easy eclecticism that adopts all forms with equal facility and betrays the decadence or the sterility of the time. I recall the fact that the city was in process of reconstruction when it was destroyed. Its unskilful repairs disclose a certain predilection for that cheap kind of elegance which among us, has taken the place of art. Stucco tricks off and disfigures everything. Reality is sacrificed to appearance, and genuine elegance to that kind of showy avarice which assumes a false look of profusion. In many places, the flutings are economically preserved by means of moulds that fill them in the lower part of the columns. Painting takes the place of sculpture at every point where it can supply it. The capitals affect odd shapes, sometimes successfully, but always at variance with the simplicity of high art. Add to these objections other faults, glaring at first glance, — for instance, the adornment of the temple of Mercury, where the panels terminate alternately in pediments and in arcades; the façade of the purgatorium in the temple of Isis, where the arcade itself cutting the cornice, becomes involved hideously with the pediment. I shall say nothing either, of the fountains, or of the columns, alas! formed of shell-work and mosaic.

Faults like these shock the eye of purists; but let us constantly bear in mind that we are in a small city, the finest residence in which belonged to a wine-merchant. We could not with fairness expect to find there the Parthenon, or even the Pantheon of Rome. The Pompeian architects worked for simple burghers whose moderate wish was to own pretty houses, not too large nor too dear, but of rich external appearance and a gayety of look that gratified the eye. These good tradesmen were served to their hearts' content by skilful persons who turned everything to good account, cutting rooms by scores within a space that would not be sufficient for one large saloon in our palaces, profiting by all the accidents of the soil to raise their structures by stories into amphitheatres, devising one ingenious subterfuge after another to mask the defects of alignment, and, in a word, with feeble resources and narrow means, realizing what the ancients always dreamed — art combined with every-day life.

For proof of this I point to their paintings covering those handsome stucco walls, which were so carefully prepared, so frequently overlaid with the finest mortar, so ingeniously dashed with shining powder, and, then, so often smoothed, repolished and repacked with wooden rollers that they, at last, looked like and passed for marble. Whether painted in fresco or *dry*, in encaustic or by other processes, matters little—that belongs to technical authorities to decide.*

---

* The learned Minervini has remarked certain differences in the washes put on the Pompeian walls. He has indicated finer ones with which, according to him, the ancients painted in fresco their more studied compositions, landscapes, and figures, while ordinary decorations were painted *dry* by inferior painters. I recall the fact, as I pass on, that several paintings, particularly the

However that may be, these mural decorations were nevertheless a feast for the eyes, and are so still. They divided the walls into five or six panels, developing themselves between a socle and a frieze; the socle being deeper, the frieze clearer in tint, the interspace of a more vivid red and yellow, for instance, while the frieze was white and the socle black. In plain houses these single panels were divided by simple lines; then gradually, as the house selected became more opulent, these lines were replaced by ornamental frames, garlands, pilasters, and, ere long, fantastic pavilions, in which the fancy of the decorative artist disported at will. However, the socles became covered with foliage, the friezes with arabesques, and the panels with paintings, the latter

---

most important, were detached, but secured to the wall with iron clamps. It has ever been noticed that the back of these pictures did not adhere to the walls—an excellent precaution against dampness. This custom of sawing off and shifting mural paintings was very ancient. It is known that the wealthy Romans adorned their houses with works of art borrowed or stolen from Greece, and all will remember the famous contract of Mummius, who, in arranging with some merchants to convey to Rome the masterpieces of Zeuxis and Apelles, stipulated that if they should be lost or damaged on the way, the merchants should replace them at their own expense.

quite simple at first, such as a flower, a fruit, a land-scape; pretty soon a figure, then a group, then at last great historical or religious subjects that sometimes covered a whole piece of wall and to which the socle and the frieze served as a sort of showy and majestic framework. Thus, the fancy of the decorator could rise even to the height of epic art.

Those paintings will be eternally studied: they give us precious data, not only on art, but concerning everything that relates to antiquity,— its manners and customs, its ceremonies, its costumes, the homes of those days, the elements and nature as they then appeared. Pompeii is not a gallery of pictures; it is rather an illustrated journal of the first century. One there sees odd landscapes; a little island on the edge of the water; a bank of the Nile where an ass, stooping to drink, bends toward the open jaws of a crocodile which he does not see, while his master frantically but vainly endeavors to pull him back by the tail. These pieces nearly always consist of rocks on the edge of the water, sometimes interspersed with trees, sometimes covered with ranges of temples, sometimes stretching away in rugged solitudes, where some

shepherd wanders astray with his flock, or from time
to time, enlivened with a historical scene (Andromeda and Perseus).   Then come little pictures of in-
animate nature, — baskets of fruit, vases of flowers,
household utensils, bunches of vegetables, the collection of office-furniture painted in the house of Lucretius (the inkstand, the stylus, the paper-knife, the tablets, and a letter folded in the shape of a napkin with
the address, "To Marcus Aurelius, flamen of Mars, and
decurion of Pompeii").   Sometimes these paintings
have a smack of humor; there are two that go together on the same wall.   One of them shows a cock
and a hen strolling about full of life, while upon the
other the cock is in durance vile, with his legs tied
and looking most doleful indeed: his hour has
come!

I say nothing of the bouquets in which lilies, the
iris, and roses predominate, nor of the festoons, the garlands, nay, the whole thickets that adorn the walls of
Sallust's garden.   Let me here merely point out
the pictures of animals, the hunting scenes, and the
combats of wild beasts, treated with such astonishing
vigor and raciness.   There is one, especially, still

quite fresh and still in its place, in one of the houses recently discovered. It represents a wild boar rushing headlong upon a bear, in the presence of a lion, who looks on at him with the most superb indifference. It is divined, as the Neapolitans say; that is, the painter has intuitively conceived the feelings of the two animals; the one blind with reckless fury, the other supremely confident in his own agility and superior strength.

And now I come to the human form. Here we have endless variety; and all kinds, from the caricature to the epic effort, are attempted and exhausted, — the wagon laden with an enormous goat-skin full of wine, which slaves are busily putting into amphoræ; a child making an ape dance; a painter copying a Hermes of Bacchus; a pensive damsel probably about to dispatch a secret message by the buxom servant-maid waiting there for it; a vendor of Cupids opening his cage full of little winged gods, who, as they escape, tease a sad and pensive woman standing near, in a thousand ways, — how many different subjects! But I have said nothing yet. The Pompeians especially excelled in fancy pictures. Everybody has

16

seen those swarms of little genii that, fluttering down upon the walls of their houses, wove crowns or garlands, angled with the rod and line, chased birds, sawed planks, planed tables, raced in chariots, or danced on the tight-rope, holding up thyrses for balancing poles; one bent over, another kneeling, a third making a jet of wine spirt forth from a horn into a vase, a fourth playing on the lyre, and a fifth on the double flute, without leaving the tight-rope that bends beneath their nimble feet. But more beautiful than these divine rope-dancers were the female dancers, who floated about, perfect prodigies of self-possession and buoyancy, rising of themselves from the ground and sustained without an effort in the voluptuous air that cradled them. You may see these all at the museum in Naples,—the nymph who clashes the cymbals, and one who drums the tambourine; another who holds aloft a branch of cedar and a golden sceptre; one who is handing a plate of figs; and her, too who has a basket on her head and a thyrsis in her hand. Another in dancing uncovers her neck and her shoulders, and a third, with her head thrown back, and her eyes uplifted to heaven, inflates her

veil as though to fly away. Here is one dropping
bunches of flowers in a fold of her robe, and there
another who holds a golden plate in this hand, while
with that she covers her brows with an undulating
pallium, like a bird putting its head under its
wing.

There are some almost nude, and some that drape
themselves in tissues quite transparent and woven of
the air. Some again wrap themselves in thick mantles which cover them completely, but which are about
to fall; two of them holding each other by the hand
are going to float upward together. As many dancing
nymphs as there are, so many are the different dances,
attitudes, movements, undulations, characteristics, and
dissimilar ways of removing and putting on veils;
infinite variations, in fine, upon two notes that vibrate
with voluptuous luxuriance, and in a thousand
ways.

Let us continue: We are sweeping into the full tide
of mythology. All the ancient divinities will pass
before us,—now isolated (like the fine, nay, truly
imposing Ceres in the house of Castor and Pollux),
now grouped in well-known scenes, some of which

often recur on the Pompeian walls. Thus, the educa
tion of Bacchus, his relations with Silenus; the roman
tic story of Ariadne; the loves of Jupiter, Apollo, and
Daphne; Mars and Venus; Adonis dying; Zephyr
and Flora; but, above all, the heroes of renown,
Theseus and Andromeda, Meleager, Jason, heads
of Hercules; his twelve labors, his combat with
the Nemæan lion, his weaknesses, — such are the
episodes most in favor with the decorative artists
of the little city. Sometimes they take their subjects from the poems of Virgil, but oftener from
those of Homer. I might cite a whole house, viz., that
of the Poet, also styled the Homeric House, the
interior court of which was a complete Iliad illustrated. There you could see the parting of Agamemnon and Chryseis, and also that of Briseis and
Achilles, who, seated on a throne, with a look of angry
resignation, is requesting the young girl to return to
Agamemnon — a fine picture, of deserved celebrity.
There, too, was beheld the lovely Venus which Gell
has not hesitated to compare, as to form, with the
Medicean statue, or for color, to Titian's painting. It
will be remembered that she plays a conspicuous part

Exedra of the House of Sirieus.

in the poem. A little further on we see Jupiter and Juno meeting on Mount Ida.

"At length" says Nicolini, in his sumptuous work on Pompeii, "in the natural sequence of these episodes, appears Thetis reclining on the Triton, and holding forth to her afflicted son the arms that Vulcan had forged for him in her presence."

It was in the peristyle of this house that the copy of the famous picture by Timanthius of the sacrifice of Iphigenia was found. "Having represented her standing near the altar on which she is to perish, the artist depicts profound grief on the faces of those who are present, especially of Menelaus; then, having exhausted all the the symbols of sorrow, he veils the father's countenance, finding it impossible to give a befitting expression." This was, according to Pliny, the work of Timanthus, and such is exactly the reproduction of it as it was found in the house of the poet at Pompeii.

This Iphigenia and the Medea in the house of Castor and Pollux, recalling the masterpiece of Timomachos the Byzantine are the only two Pompeian pictures which reproduce well-known paintings;

16*

but let us not, for that reason, conclude that the others are original. The painters of the little city were neither creators nor copyists, but very free imitators, varying familiar subjects to suit themselves. Hence, that variety which surprises us in their reproductions of the same subject. Indeed, I have seen, at least ten Ariadnes surprised by Bacchus, and there are no two alike. Hence, also, that ease and freedom of touch indicating that the decorative artists executing them felt quite at their ease. Assuredly, their efforts, which are of quite unequal merit, are not models of correctness by any means; faults of drawing and proportion, traits of awkardness and heedlessness, swarm in them; but let anybody pick out a sub-prefecture of 30,000 inhabitants, in France, and say to the painters of the district: "Here, my good friends, just go to work and tear off those sheets of colored paper that you find pasted upon the walls of rooms and saloons in every direction, and paint there in place of them socles and friezes, devotional images, *genre* pictures, and historical pieces summing up the ideas, creeds, manners and tastes, of our time in such sort that were the Pyrenees, the Cevennes, or the Jura Alps, to crum-

ble upon you to-morrow, future generations, on digging up your houses and your masterpieces, might there
study the life of our period although it will be antiquity for them." . . . What would the painters
of the place be apt to do or say? I think I may reply,
with all respect to them, that they would at least be
greatly embarrassed.

But, on their part, the Pompeians were not a whit
put out when they came to repaint their whole city
afresh. Would you like to get an accurate idea of
their real merit and their indisputable value? If so,
ask some one to conduct you through the houses that
have been lately exhumed, and look at the paintings
still left in their places as they appear with all the
brilliance that Vesuvius has preserved in them, and
which the sunlight will soon impair. In the saloon of
the house of Proculus notice two pieces that correspond, namely, Narcissus and the Triumph of Bacchus — powerless languor and victorious activity. The
intended meaning is clearly apparent, and is simply
and vividly rendered. The ancients never required
commentators to make them understood. You comprehend their idea and their subject at first glance.

The most ignorant of men and the least versed in
Pagan lore, take their meaning with half a look and
give their works a title. In them we find no beating
about the bush, no circumlocution, no hidden mean-
ings, no confusion; the painter expresses what he
means, does it quickly and does it well, without exag-
gerating his terms or overloading the scene. His
principal personages stand out boldly, yet the accessories do not cry aloud, "Look at me!" The picture of
Narcissus represents Narcissus first and foremost;
then it brings in a solitude and a streamlet. The
coloring has a brilliance and harmoniousness of tint
that surprises us, but there are no useless effects in it.
In nearly all these frescoes (excepting the wedding of
Zephyrus and Flora) the light spreads over it, white
and equable (no one says cold and monotonous), for its
office is not merely to illuminate the picture, but to
throw sufficient glow and warmth upon the wall.
The low and narrow rooms having, instead of windows,
only a door opening on the court, had need of this
painted daylight which skilful pencils wrought
for them. And what movement there was in all

Exedra of the House of Siricus (See p. 195).

those figures, what suppleness and what truth to nature! *

Nothing is distorted, nothing attitudinizes. Ariadne is really asleep, and Hercules, in wine, really sinks to the ground; the dancing girl floats in the air as though in her native element; the centaur gallops without an effort; it is simple *reality* — the very reverse of realism — natuie such as she actually is when she is pleasant to behold, in the full effusion of her grace, advancing like a queen because she *is* a queen, and because she could not move in any other fashion. In a word, these second-rate painters, poor daubers of walls as they were, had, in the absence of scientific skill and correctness, the flash of latent genius in obscurity, the instinct of art, spontaneousness, freedom of touch, and vivid life.

Such were the walls of Pompeii. Let us now glance at the pavements. They will astonish us much more. At the outset the pavements were quite plain.

---

* "And how the ancients, even the most unskilful, understood the right treatment of nude subjects!" said an eminent critic to me, one day, as he was with me admiring these pictures; "and," he added, "we know nothing more about it now; *our* statues are not nude, but undressed."

There was a cement formed of a kind of mortar; this was then thoroughly dusted with pulverized brick, and the whole converted into a composition, which, when it had hardened, was like red granite. Many rooms and courts at Pompeii are paved with this composition which was called *opus signinum*. Then, in this crust, they at first ranged small cubes of marble, of glass, of calcareous stone, of colored enamel, forming squares or stripes, then others complicating the lines or varying the colors, and others again tracing regular designs, meandering lines, and arabesques, until the divided pebbles at length completely covered the reddish basis, and thus they finally became mosaics, those carpetings of stone which soon rose to the importance and value of great works of art.

The house of the Faun at Pompeii, which is the most richly paved of all, was a museum of mosaics. There was one before the door, upon the sidewalk, inscribed with the ancient salutation, *Salve!* Another, at the end of the prothyrum, artistically represented masks. Others again, in the wings of the atrium, made up a little menagerie, — a brace of ducks, dead birds, shell-work, fish, doves taking pearls from a casket, and a cat devouring a quail — a perfect master-piece of living movement and precision. Pliny mentions a house, the flooring of which represented the fragments of a meal: it was called *the ill-swept house.* But let us not quit the house of the Faun, where the mosaic-workers had, besides what we have told, wrought on the pavement of the œcus a superb lion foreshortened — much worn away, indeed, but marvellous for vigor and boldness. In the triclinium another mosaic represented Acratus, the Bacchic genius, astride of a panther; lastly the piece in the exædra, the finest that exists, is counted among the most precious specimens of ancient art. It is the famous battle of Arbelles or of Issus. A squadron of Greeks, already victorious, is rushing upon the Persians; Alexander is galloping at the head of his cavalry. He has lost his helmet in the heat of the charge, his horses' manes stand erect, and his long spear has pierced the leader of the enemy. The Persians, overthrown and routed, are turning to flee; those who immediately surround Darius, the vanquished king, think of nothing but their own safety; but Darius is totally forgetful of himself. His hand extended toward his dying general, he turns his back to the flying rabble and seems to invite death. The whole scene — the head-long rush of the one army, the utter confusion of the other, the chariot of the King wheeling to the front, the rage, the terror, the pity expressed, and all this profoundly felt and clearly rendered — strikes the beholder at first glance and engraves itself upon his memory, leaving there the imperishable impression that masterpieces in art can alone produce. And yet this wonderful work was but the flooring of a saloon! The ancients put their feet where we put our hands, says an Englishman who utters but the simple truth. The finest tables in the palaces at Naples were cut from the pavements in the houses at Pompeii.

It was in the same dwelling that the celebrated bronze statuette of the Dancing Faun was found. It has its head and arms uplifted, its shoulders thrown back, its breast projecting, every muscle in motion, the whole body dancing. An accompanying piece, however, was lacking to this little deity so full of spring and vigor, and that piece has been exhumed by recent excavations, in quite an humble tenement. It represents a delicate youth, full of nonchalance and grace, a Narcissus hearkening to the musical echo in the distance. His head leans over, his ear is stretched to listen, his finger is turned in the direction whence he hears the sound — his whole body listens. Placed near each other in the museum, these two bronzes would make Pagans of us were religion but an affair of art.*

Then the mere wine-merchants of a little ancient city adorned their fountains with treasures like these! Others have been found, less precious, perhaps, but charming, nevertheless; the fisherman in sitting posture at the small mosaic fountain; the group representing Hercules holding a stag bent over his knee; a diminutive Apollo leaning, lyre in hand, against a pillar; an aged Silenus carrying a goat-skin of wine; a pretty Venus arranging her moistened tresses; a hunting Diana, etc.; without counting the Hermes and the double busts, one among the rest comprising the two heads of a male and female Faun full of intemperance and coarse gayety. 'Tis true that everything is not perfect in these sculptures, par-

---

* Recently, Signor Fiorelli has found another bronze statuette of a bent and crooked Silenus worth both the others.

17

ticularly in the marbles. The statues of Livia, of
Drusus, and of Eumachia, are but moderately good;
those discovered in the temples, such as Isis, Bacchus,
Venus, etc., have not come down from the Parthenon.
The decline of taste makes itself apparent in the
latest ornamentation of the tombs and edifices, and
the decorative work of the houses, the marble em-
bellishments; and, above all, those executed in stucco
become overladen and tawdry, heavy and labored,
toward the last. Nevertheless, they reveal, if not
a great æsthetic feeling, at least that yearning for
elegance which entered so profoundly into the manners of the ancients. With us, in fine, art is never
anything but a superfluity—something unfamiliar
and foreign that comes in to us from the outside
when we are wealthy. Our paintings and our
sculptures do not make part and parcel of our
houses. If we have a Venus of Milo on our mantel-
clock, it is not because we worship beauty, nor that,
to our view, there is the slightest connection
between the mother of the Graces and the hour of
the day. Venus finds herself very much out of her

element there; she is in exile, evidently. On the other hand, at Pompeii she is at home, as Saint Genevieve once was at Paris, as Saint Januarius still is at Naples. She was the venerated patroness whose protection they invoked, whose anger they feared. "May the wrath of the angry Pompeian Venus fall upon him!" was their form of imprecation. All these well-known stories of gods and demigods who throned it on the walls, were the fairy tales, the holy legends, the thousand-times-repeated narratives that delighted the Pompeians. They had no need of explanatory programmes when they entered their domestic museums. To find something resembling this state of things, we should have to go into our country districts where there still reigns a divinity of other days—Glory—and admiringly observe with what religious devotion coarse lithographs of the "Old Flag," and of the "Little Corporal," are there retained and cherished. There, and there only, our modern art has infused itself into the life and manners of the people. Is it equal to ancient art?

If, from painting and sculpture, we descend to inferior branches, — if, as we tried to do in the house of Pansa, we despoil the museum so as to restore their inmates to the homes of Pompeii, and put back in its place the fine candelabra with the carved panther bearing away the infant Bacchus at full speed; the precious *scyphus,* in which two centaurs take a bevy of little Cupids on their cruppers; that other vase on which Pallas is standing erect in a car, leaning on her spear; the silver saucepan, — there were such in those days, — the handle of which is secured by two birds' heads; the simple pair of scales — they carved scales. then! — where one sees the half bust of a warrior wearing a splendid helmet; in fine, the humblest articles, utensils of lowest use, nay, even simple earthenware covered with graceful ornaments, sometimes exquisitely worked; — were we to go to the museum at Naples and ask what the ancients used instead of the hideous boxes in which we shut up our dead, and there behold this beautiful urn which looks as though it were incrusted with ivory, and which has upon it in bas-relief carved masks enveloped in complicated

vine-tendrils twisted, laden with clusters of grapes,
intermingled with other foliage, tangled all up in rol-
licking arabesques, forming rosettes, in the midst of
which birds are seen perching, and leaving but two
spaces open where children dear to Bacchus are pluck-
ing grapes or treading them under foot, trilling
stringed lyres, blowing on double flutes or tumbling
about and snapping their fingers — the urn itself in
blue glass and the reliefs in white — for the ancients
knew how to carve glass, — ah! undoubtedly, in sur-
veying all these marvels, we should be forced to con-
cede that the citizen in old times was at least, as
much of an artist as he is to-day. This was because
in those times no barrier was erected between the
citizen and the artist. There were no two opposing
camps — on one side the Philistines, and on the other
the people of God. There was no line of distinction
between the needful and the superfluous, between the
positive and the ideal. Art was daily bread, and not
holiday pound-cake; it made its way everywhere; it
illuminated, it gladdened, it perfumed everything.
It did not stand either outside of or above ordinary
life; it was the soul and the delight of life; in a word,

17*

it penetrated it, and was penetrated by it, — it *lived!*
This is what these modest ruins teach.*

* A badly interpreted inscription on the gate of Nola had led, for
a moment, to the belief that the importation of this singular worship dated back to the early days of the little city; but we now
know that it was introduced by Sylla into the Roman world.   Isis
was Nature, the patroness of the Pompeians, who venerated her
equally in their physical Venus.   This form of religion, mysterious,
symbolical, full of secrets hidden from the people, as it was; these
goddesses with heads of dogs, wolves, oxen, hawks; the god Onion,
the god Garlic, the god Leek; all that Apuleius tells about it, besides the data furnished by the Pompeian excavations, the recov-
ered bottle-brushes, the basins, the knives, the tripods, the cymbals, the citheræ, etc., — were worth the trouble of examination
and study.

Upon the door of the temple, a strange inscription announced
that Numerius Popidius, the son of Numerius, had, at his own expense, rebuilt the temple of Isis, thrown down by an earthquake,
and that, in reward for his liberality, the decurions had admitted
him gratuitously to their college at the age of six years.   The antiquaries, or some of them, at least, finding this age improbable,
have read it sixty instead of six, forgetting that there then existed
two kinds of decurions, the *ornamentarii* and *prætextati* — the honorary and the active officials.   The former might be associated
with the Pompeian Senate in recompense for services rendered by
their fathers.   An inscription found at Misenum confirms this fact.
(See the *Memorie del l'Academia Ercolanese, anno* 1833) — The
minutes of the Herculaneum Academy, for the year 1833.

VIII.

THE THEATRES.

We are now going to rest ourselves at the theatre. Pompeii had two such places of amusement, one tragic and the other comic, or, rather, one large and one smaller, for that is the only positive difference existing between them; all else on that point is pure hypothesis. Let us, then, say the large and small theatre, and we shall be sure to make no mistakes.

The grand saloon or body of the large theatre formed a semicircle, built against an embankment so that the tiers of seats ascended from the pit to the topmost gallery, without resting on massive

substructures. In this respect it was of Greek construction. The four upper tiers resting upon an
arched corridor, in the Roman style, alone reached
the height on which stood the triangular Forum
and the Greek temple. Thus, you can step directly
from the level of the street to the highest galleries,
from which your gaze, ranging above the stage,
can sweep the country and the sea, and at the same
moment plunge far below you into that sort of
regularly-shaped ravine in which once sat five thousand Pompeians eager for the show.

At first glance, you discover three main divisions;
these are the different ranks of tiers, the *caveæ*.
There are three caveæ—the lowermost, the middle, and the upper ones. The lowermost was considered the most select. It comprised only the four
first rows of benches, or seats, which were broader
and not so high as the others. These were the
places reserved for magistrates and other eminent
persons. Thither they had their seats carried and
also the *bisellia*, or benches for two persons, on
which they alone had the right to sit. A low wall,
rising behind the fourth range and surmounted with

a marble rail that has now disappeared, separated
this lowermost cavea from the rest. The duumviri,
the decurions, the augustales, the ædiles, Holconius,
Cornelius Rufus, and Pansa, if he was elected, sat
there majestically apart from common mortals. The
middle division was for quiet, every-day, private citizens, like ourselves. Separated into wedge-like corners
(*cunei*) by six flights of steps cutting it in as many
places, it comprised a limited number of seats marked
by slight lines, still visible. A ticket of admission
(a *tessera* or domino) of bone, earthenware, or
bronze — a sort of counter cut in almond or *en pigeon*
shape, sometimes too in the form of a ring — indicated
exactly the cavea, the corner, the tier, and the seat
for the person holding it. Tessaræ of this kind
have been found on which were Greek and Roman
characters (a proof that the Greek would not have
been understood without translation). Upon one of
them is inscribed the name of Æschylus, in the genitive; and hence it has been inferred that his "Pro-
metheus" or his "Persians" must have been played
on the Pompeian stage, unless, indeed, this genitive
designated one of the wedge-divisions marked out

by the name or the statue of the tragic poet. Others
have mentioned one of these counters that announced
the representation of a piece by Plautus, — the *Cas-
ina;* but I can assure you that the relic is a forgery,
if, indeed, such a one ever existed.

You should, then, before entering, provide yourself
with a real tessera, which you may purchase for very
little money. Plautus asked that folks should pay an
as apiece. "Let those," he said, "who have not got it
retire to their homes." The price of the seats was
proclaimed aloud by a crier, who also received the
money, unless the show was gratuitously offered to the
populace by some magistrate who wished to retain
public favor, or some candidate anxious to procure it.
You handed in your ticket to a sort of usher, called
the *designator*, or the *locarius*, who pointed out your
seat to you, and, if required, conducted you thither.
You could then take your place in the middle tier, at
the top of which was the statue of Marcus Holconius
Rufus, duumvir, military tribune, and patron of the
colony. This statue had been set up there by order
of the decurions. The holes hollowed in the pedestal

by the nails that secured the marble feet of the statue are still visible.

Finally, at the summit of the half-moon was the uppermost cavea, assigned to the common herd and the women. So, after all, we are somewhat ahead of the Romans in gallantry. Railings separated this tier from the one we sit in, so as to prevent "the low rabble" from invading the seats occupied by us respectable men of substance. Upon the wall of the people's gallery is still seen the ring that held the pole of the *velarium*. This velarium was an awning that was stretched above the heads of the spectators to protect them from the sun. In earlier times the Romans had scouted at this innovation, which they called a piece of Campanian effeminacy. But little by little, increasing luxury reduced the Puritans of Rome to silence, and they willingly accepted a velarium of silk — an homage of Cæsar. Nero, who carried everything to excess, went further: he caused a velarium of purple to be embroidered with gold. Caligula frequently amused himself by suddenly withdrawing this movable shelter and leaving the naked heads of the spectators exposed to the beating rays of the sun.

But it seems that at Pompeii the wind frequently pre-
vented the hoisting of the canvas, and so the poet
Martial tells us that he will keep on his hat.

Such was the arrangement of the main body of the
house. Let us now descend to the orchestra, which,
in the Greek theatres, was set apart for the dancing of
the choirs, but in the Roman theatres, was reserved for
the great dignitaries, and at Rome itself for the prince,
the vestals, and the senators. I have somewhere
read that, in the great city, the foreign ambassadors
were excluded from these places of honor because
among them could be found the sons of freedmen.

Would you like to go up on the stage? Raised
about five feet above the orchestra, it was broader than
ours, but not so deep. The personages of the antique
repertory did not swell to such numbers as in our
fairy spectacles. Far from it. The stage extended
between a proscenium or front, stretching out upon the
orchestra by means of a wooden platform, which has
disappeared, and the *postscenium* or side scenes.
There was, also, a *hyposcenium* or subterranean part
of the theatre, for the scene-shifters and machinists.
The curtain or *siparium* (a Roman invention) did not

rise to the ceiling as with us, but, on the contrary, descended so as to disclose the stage, and rolled together underground, by means of ingenious processes which Mazois has explained to us. Thus, the curtain fell at the beginning and rose at the end of the piece.

You are aware that in ancient drama the question of scenery was greatly simplified by the rule of the unity of place. The stage arrangement, for instance, represented the palace of a prince. Therefore, there was no canvas painted at the back of the stage; it was *built* up. This decoration, styled the *scena stabilis*, rose as high as the loftiest tier in the theatre, and was of stone and marble in the Pompeian edifice. It represented a magnificent wall pierced for three doors; in the centre was the royal door, where princes entered; on the right, the entrance of the household and females; at the left, the entrance for guests and strangers. These were matters to be fixed in the mind of the spectator. Between these doors were rounded and square niches for statues. In the side-scenes, was the moveable decoration (*scena ductilis*), which was slid in front of the back-piece in case of

18

a change of scene, as, for instance, when playing the *Ajax* of Sophocles, where the place of action is transferred from the Greek camp to the shores of the Hellespont. Then, there were other side-scenes not of much account, owing to lack of room, and on each wing a turning piece with three broad flats representing three different subjects. There were square niches in the walls of the proscenium either for statues or for policemen to keep an eye on the spectators. Such, stated in a few lines and in libretto style, was the stage in ancient times.

I confess that I have a preference for the smaller theatre which has been called the Odeon. Is that because, possibly, tragedies were never played there? Is it because this establishment seems more complete and in better preservation, thanks to the intelligent replacements of La Vega, the architect? It was covered, as two inscriptions found there explicitly declare, with a wooden roof, probably, the walls not being strong enough to sustain an arch. It was reached through a passage all bordered with inscriptions, traced on the walls by the populace waiting to secure admission as they passed slowly in, one after

The Smaller Theatre at Pompeii.

the other. A lengthy file of gladiators had carved their names also upon the walls, along with an enumeration of their victories; barbarian slaves, and some freedmen, likewise, had left their marks. These probably constituted the audience that occupied the uppermost seats approached by the higher vomitories. On the other hand, there were no lateral vomitories. The spectators entered the orchestra directly by large doors, and thence ascended to the four tiers of the lower (*cavea*) which curved like hooks at their extremities, and were separated from the middle cavea by a parapet of marble terminating in vigorously-carved lion's paws. Among these carvings we may particularly note a crouching Atlas, of short, thick-set form, sustaining on his shoulders and his arms, which are doubled behind him, a marble slab which was once the stand of a vase or candlestick. This athletic effort is violently rendered by the artist. Above the orchestra ran the *tribunalia*, reminding us of our modern stage-boxes. These were the places reserved at Rome for the vestal virgins; at Pompeii, they were very probably those of the public priestesses — of Eumachia, whose statue we have already seen, or of Mamia whose tomb we have inspected. The seats of the three cavea were of blocks of lava; and there can still be seen in them the hollows in which the occupants placed their feet so as not to soil the spectators below them. Let us remember that the Roman mantles were of white wool, and that the sandals of the ancients got muddied just as our shoes do. The citizens who occupied the central cavea brought their cushions with them or folded their spotless togas on the seats before they took their places. It was necessary, then, to protect them from the mud and the dust in which the spectators occupying the upper tiers had been walking.

The number of ranges of seats was seventeen, divided into wedges by six flights of steps, and in stalls by lines yet visible upon the stone. The upper tiers were approached by vomitories and by a subterranean corridor. The orchestra formed an arc the chord of which was indicated by a marble strip with this inscription:

"M. Olconius M. F. Vervs, Pro Ludis."

This Olconius or Holconius was the Marquis of Carabas of Pompeii. His name may be read everywhere in the streets, on the monuments, and on the walls of the houses. We have seen already that the fruiterers wanted him for ædile. We have pointed out the position of his statue in the theatre. We know by inscriptions that he was not the only illustrious member of his family. There were also a Marcus Holconius Celer, a Marcus Holconius Rufus, etc. Were this petty municipal aristocracy worth the trouble of hunting up, we could easily find it on the electoral programmes by collecting the names usually affixed thereon. But Holconius is the one most conspicuous of them all; so, hats off to Holconius!

I return to the theatre. Two large side windows illuminated the stage, which, being covered, had need of light. The back scene was not carved, but painted and pierced for five doors instead of three; those at the ends, which were masked by movable side scenes served, perhaps, as entrances to the lobbies of the priestesses.

Would you like to go behind the scenes? Passing by the barracks of the gladiators, we enter an apartment adorned with columns, which was, very likely, the common hall and dressing-room of the actors. A celebrated mosaic in the house of the poet (or jew-

18*

cller), shows us a scenic representation : in it we observe the *choragus*, surrounded by masks and other accessories (the choragus was the manager and director); he is making two actors, got up as satyrs, rehearse their parts; behind them, another comedian, assisted by a costumer of some kind, is trying to put on a yellow garment which is too small for him. Thus we can re-people the antechamber of the stage. We see already those comic masks that were the principal resource in the wardrobe of the ancient players. Some of them were typical; for instance, that of the young virgin, with her hair parted on her forehead and carefully combed; that of the slave-driver (or *hegemonus*), recognized by his raised eyelids, his wrinkled brows and his twists of hair done up in a wig; that of the wizard, with immense eyes starting from their sockets, seamed skin covered with pimples, with enormous ears, and short hair frizzed in snaky ringlets; that of the bearded, furious, staring, and sinister old man; and above all, those of the Atellan low comedians, who, born in Campania, dwell there still, and must assuredly have amused the little city through which we are passing. Atella, the country of Maccus was only some seven or eight leagues distant from Pompeii, and numerous interests and business connections united the inhabitants of the two places. I have frequently stated that the Oscan language, in which the Atellan farces were written, had once been the only tongue, and had continued to be the popular dialect of the Pompeians. The Latin gradually intermingled with these pieces, and the confusion of the two idioms was an exhaustless source of witticisms, puns, and bulls of all kinds, that must have afforded Homeric laughter to the plebeians of Pompeii. The longshoremen of Naples, in our day, seek exactly similar effects in the admixture of pure Italian and the local *patois*. The titles of some of the Atellian farces are still extant: "Pappus, the Doctor Shown Out," "Maccus Married," "Maccus as Safe Keeper," etc. These are nearly the same subjects that are still treated every day on the boards at Naples; the same rough daubs, half improvised on the spur of the moment; the same frankly coarse and indecent gayety. The Odeon where we are now, was the Pompeian San Carlino. Bucco, the stupid and mocking buffoon; the dotard Pappus, who reminds us of the Venetian

Pantaloon; Mandacus, who is the Neapolitan Guappo; the Oscan Casnar, a first edition of Cassandra; and finally, Maccus, the king of the company, the Punchinello who still survives and flourishes,—such were the ancient mimes, and such, too, are their modern successors. All these must have appeared in their turn on the small stage of the Odeon; and the slaves, the freedmen crowded together in the upper tiers, the citizens ranged in the middle cavea or family-circle, the duumvirs, the decurions, the augustals, the ædiles seated majestically on the bisellia of the orchestra, even the priestesses of the proscenium and the melancholy Eumachia, whose statue confesses, I know not what anguish of the heart,—all these must have roared with laughter at the rude and extravagant sallies of their low comedians, who, notwithstanding the parts they played, were more highly appreciated than the rest and had the exclusive privilege of wearing the title of Roman citizens.

Now, if these trivialities revolt your fastidious taste, you can picture to yourself the representation of some comedy of Plautus in the Odeon of Pompeii; that is, admitting, to begin with, that you can find a comedy

by that author which in no wise shocks our susceptibili·
ties.   You can also fill the stage with mimes and pan·
tomimists, for the favor accorded to that class of actors
under the emperors is well known.   The Cæsars — I
am speaking of the Romans—somewhat feared spoken
comedy, attributing political proclivities to it, as they
did ; and, hence, they encouraged to their utmost that
mute comedy which, at the same time, in the Imperial
Babel, had the advantage of being understood by all
the   conquered nations.   In   the provinces, this supreme art of gesticulation, "these talking fingers, these
loquacious hands, this voluble silence, this unspoken
explanation," as was once choicely said, were service-
able in advancing the great work of Roman unity.
"The substitution of ballet pantomimes for comedy and
tragedy resulted in causing the old masterpieces to be
neglected, thereby enfeebling the practice of the
national idioms and seconding the propagation, if not
of the language, at least of the customs and ideas of
the Romans."   (Charles Magnin.)

If the mimes do not suffice, call into the Odeon the
rope-dancers, the acrobats, the jugglers, the ventrilo-
quists,— for all these lower orders of public performers

existed among the ancients and swarmed in the Pompeian pictures, — or the flute-players enlivening the
waits with their melody and accompanying the voice
of the actors at moments of dramatic climax. "How
can he feel afraid," asked Cicero, in this connection,
"since he recites such fine verses while he accompanies
himself on the flute?" What would the great orator
have said had he been present at our melodramas?

We may then imagine what kind of play we please
on the little Pompeian stage. For my part, I prefer
the Atellan farces. They were the buffooneries of the
locality, the coarse pleasantry of native growth, the
hilarity of the vineyard and the grain-field, exuberant
fancy, grotesque in solemn earnest; in a word, ideal
sport and frolic without the least regard to reality —
in fine, Punchinello's comedy. We prefer Moliere; but
how many things there are in Moliere which come in
a direct line from Maccus!

It is time to leave the theatre. I have said that the
Odeon opened into the gladiators' barracks. These
barracks form a spacious court — a sort of cloister
— surrounded by seventy-four pillars, unfortunately
spoiled by the Pompeians of the restoration period.

They topped them with new capitals of stucco notoriously ill adapted to them. This gallery was surrounded with curious dwellings, among which was a prison where three skeletons were found, with their legs fastened in irons of ingeniously cruel device. The instrument in question may be seen at the museum. It looks like a prostrate ladder, in which the limbs of the prisoners were secured tightly between short and narrow rungs — four bars of iron. These poor wretches had to remain in a sitting or reclining posture, and perished thus, without the power to rise or turn over, on the day when Vesuvius swallowed up the city.

It was for a long time thought that these barracks were the quarters of the soldiery, because arms were found there; but the latter were too highly ornamented to belong to practical fighting troops, and were the very indications that suggested to Father Garrucci the firmly established idea, that the dwellings surrounding the gallery must have been occupied by gladiators. These habitations consist of some sixty cells: now there were sixty gladiators in Pompeii because an album programme announced thirty pair of them to fight in the amphitheatre.

The pillars of the gallery were covered with inscriptions scratched on their surface. Many of these graphites formed simple Greek names Pompaios, Arpokrates, Celsa, etc., or Latin names, or fragments of sentences, *curate pecunias, fur es Torque, Rustico feliciter!* etc. Others proved clearly that the place was inhabited by gladiators: *inludus Velius* (that is to say *not in the game, out of the ring*) *bis victor libertus— —leonibus, victor Veneri parmam feret.* Other inscriptions designate families or troops of gladiators, of which there are a couple familiar to us already, that of N. Festus Ampliatus and that of N. Popidius Rufus; and a third, with which we are not acquainted, namely, that of Pomponius Faustinus.

What has not been written concerning the gladiators? The origin of their bloody sports; the immolations, voluntary at first, and soon afterward compulsory, that did honor to the ashes of the dead warriors; then the combats around the funeral pyres; then, ere long, the introduction of these funeral spectacles as part of the public festivals, especially in the triumphal parades of victorious generals; then into private pageants, and then into the banquets of tyrants who caused the heads of the proscribed to be brought to them at table. The skill of such and such an artist in decapitation (*decollandi artifex*) was the subject of remark and compliment. Ah, those were the grand ages!

As the reader also knows, the gladiators were at first prisoners of war, barbarians; then, prisoners not coming in sufficient number, condemned culprits and slaves were employed, ere long, in hosts so strong as, to revolt in Campania at the summons of Spartacus. Consular armies were vanquished and the Roman prisoners, transformed to gladiators, in their turn were compelled to butcher each other around the funeral pyres of their chiefs. However, these combats had gradually ceased to be penalties and punishments, and soon were nothing but barbarous spectacles, violent pantomimic performances, like those which England and Spain have not yet been able to suppress. The troops of mercenary fighters slaughtered each other in the arenas to amuse the Romans (not to render them warlike).

19

Citizens took part in these tournaments, and among them even nobles, emperors, and women; and, at last, the Samnites, Gauls, and Thracians, who descended into the arena, were only Romans in disguise. These shows became more and more varied; they were diversified with hunts (*venationes*), in which wild beasts fought with each other or against *bestiarii*, or Christians; the amphitheatres, transformed to lakes, offered to the gaze of the delighted spectator real naval battles, and ten thousand gladiators were let loose against each other by the imperial caprice of Trajan. These entertainments lasted one hundred and twenty-three days. Imagine the carnage!

Part of the gladiators of Pompeii were Greeks, and part were real barbarians. The traces that they have left in the little city show that they got along quite merrily there. 'Tis true that they could not live, as they did at Rome, in close intimacy with emperors and empresses, but they were, none the less, the spoiled pets of the residents of Pompeii. Lodged in a sumptuous barrack, they must have been objects of envy to many of the

population. The walls are full of inscriptions con
cerning them; the bathing establishments, the inns,
and the disreputable haunts, transmit their names to
posterity. The citizens, their wives, and even their
children admired them. In the house of Proculus,
at no great height above the ground, is a picture of
a gladiator which must have been daubed there by
the young lad of the house. The gladiator whose
likeness was thus given dwelt in the house. His
helmet was found there. So, then, he was the guest
of the family, and Heaven knows how they feasted
him, petted him, and listened to him.

In order to see the gladiators under arms, we
must pass over the part of the city that has not yet
been uncovered, and through vineyards and orchards,
until, in a corner of Pompeii, as though down in
the bottom of a ravine, we find the amphitheatre.
It is a circus, surrounded by tiers of seats and abutting
on the city ramparts. The exterior wall is not high,
because the amphitheatre had to be hollowed out in
the soil. One might fancy it to be a huge vessel
deeply embedded in the sand. In this external wall
there remain two large arcades and four flights of

steps ascending to the top of the structure. The arena was so called because of the layer of sand which covered it and imbibed the blood.

It is reached by two large vaulted and paved corridors with a quite steep inclination. One of these is strengthened with seven arches that support the weight of the tiers. Both of them intersect a transverse, circular corridor, beyond which they widen. It was through this that the armed gladiators, on horseback and on foot, poured forth into the arena, to the sound of trumpets and martial music, and made the circuit of the amphitheatre before entering the lists. They then retraced their steps and came in again, in couples, according to the order of combat.

To the right of the principal entrance a doorway opens into two square rooms with gratings, where the wild beasts were probably kept. Another very narrow corridor ran from the street to the arena, near which it ascended, by a small staircase, to a little round apartment apparently the *spoliatorium*, where they stripped the dead gladiators. The arena formed an oval of sixty-eight yards by thirty-six. It was surrounded by a wall of two yards in height, above

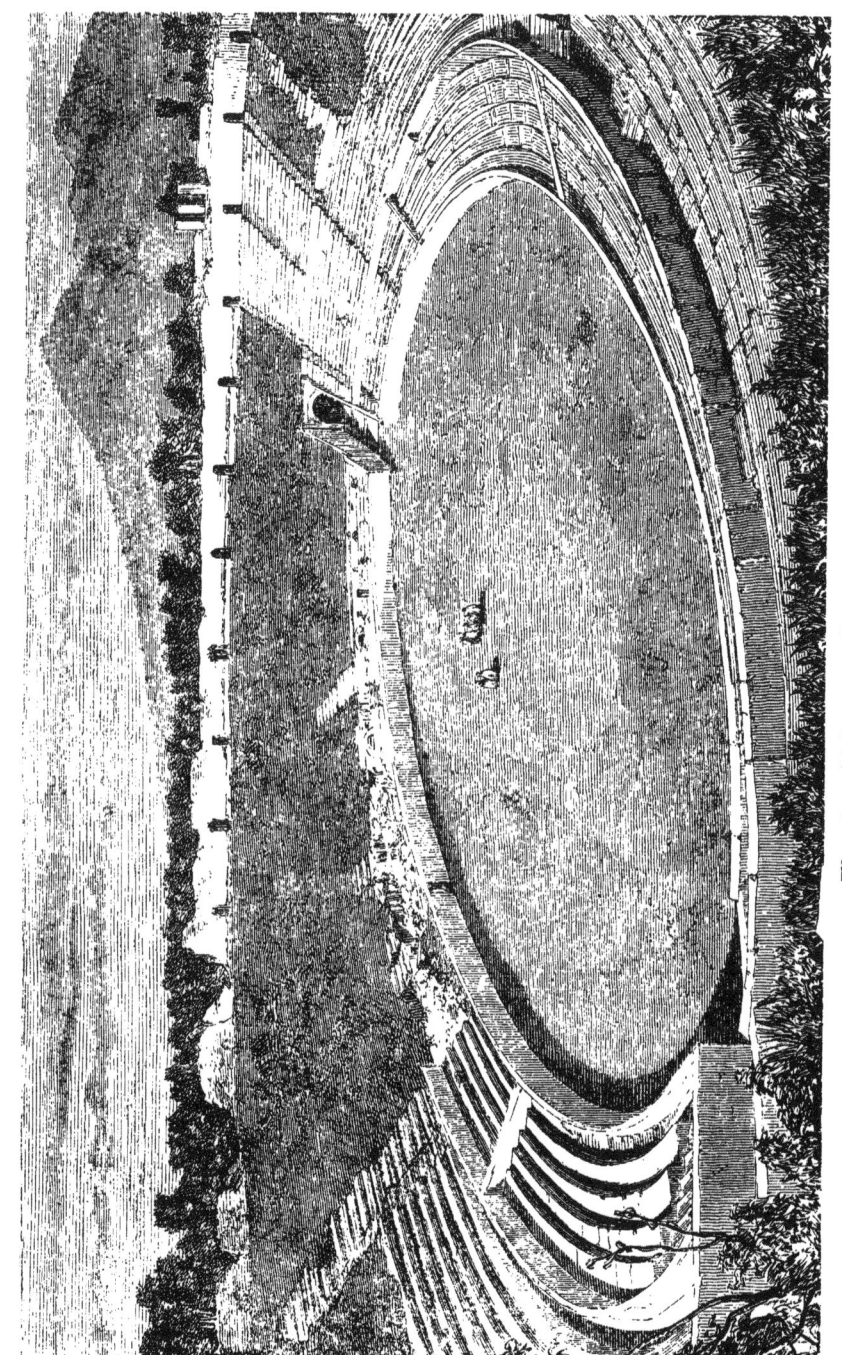

The Amphitheatre of Pompeii.

which may still be seen the holes where gratings and thick iron bars were inserted as a precaution against the bounds of the panthers. In the large amphitheatres a ditch was dug around this rampart and filled with water to intimidate the elephants, as the ancients believed them to have a horror of that element.

Paintings and inscriptions covered the walls or podium of the arena. These inscriptions acquaint us with the names of the duumvirs, — N. Istadicius, A. Audius, O. Caesctius Saxtus Capito, M. Gantrius Marcellus, who, instead of the plays and the illumination, which they would have had to pay for, on assuming office, had caused three cunei to be constructed on the order of the decurions. Another inscription gives us to understand that two other duumvirs, Caius Quinctius Valgus and Marcus Portius, holding five-year terms, had instituted the first games at their expense for the honor of the colony, and had granted the ground on which the amphitheatre stood, in perpetuity. These two magistrates must have been very generous men, and very fond of public shows. We know that they contributed, in like manner, to the construction of the Odeon.

Would you now like to go over the general sweep of the tiers—the *visorium?* Three grand divisions as in the theatre; the lowermost separated, by entries and private flights of steps, into eighteen boxes; the middle and upper one divided into cunei, the first by twenty stairways, the second by forty. Around the latter was an inclosing wall, intersected by vomitories and forming a platform where a number of spectators, arriving too late for seats, could still find standing-room, and where the manœuvres were executed that were requisite to hoist the velarium, or awning. All these made up an aggregate of twenty-four ranges of seats, upon which were packed perhaps twenty thousand spectators. So much for the audience. Nothing could be more simple or more ingenious than the system of extrication by which the movement, to and fro, of this enormous throng was made possible, and easy. The circular and vaulted corridor which, under the tiers, ran around the arena and conducted, by a great number of distinct stairways, to the tiers of the lower and middle cavea, while upper stairways enabled the populace to ascend to the highest story assigned to it.

One is surprised so see so large an amphitheatre in so small a city. But, let us not forget that Pompeii attracted the inhabitants of the neighboring towns to her festivals; history even tells us an anecdote on this subject that is not without its moral.

The Senator Liveneius Regulus, who had been driven from Rome and found an asylum in Pompeii, offered a gladiator show to the hospitable little city. A number of people from Nocera had gone to the pageant, and a quarrel arose, probably owing to municipal rivalries, that eternal curse of Italy; from words they came to blows and volleys of stones, and even to slashing with swords. There were dead and wounded on both sides. The Nocera visitors, being less numerous, were beaten, and made complaint to Rome. The affair was submitted to the Emperor, who sent it to the Senate, who referred it to the Consuls, who referred it back again to the Senate. Then came the sentence, and public shows were prohibited in Pompeii for the space of ten years. A caricature which recalls this punishment has been found in the Street of Mercury. It represented an armed gladiator descending, with a palm in his hand, into the amphitheatre: on the left, a second personage is drawing a third toward him on a seat; the third one had his arms bound, and was, no doubt, a prisoner. This inscription accompanies the entire piece: "Campanians, your victory has been as fatal to you as it was to the people of Nocera."*

The hand of Rome, ever the hand of Rome!

For that matter, the ordinances relating to the amphitheatre applied to the whole empire. One of the Pompeian inscriptions announces that the duumvir C. Cuspius Pansa had been appointed to superintend the public shows and see to the observance of the Petronian law. This law prohibited Senators from fighting in the arena, and even from sending slaves thither who had not been condemned for crime. Such things, then, required to be prohibited!

I have described the arena and the seats; let me now pass on to the show itself. Would you like to have a hunt or a gladiatorial combat? Here I invent

* M. Campfleury has reproduced this design in his very curious book on *Antique Caricature*

nothing. I have data, found at Pompeii (the paintings in the amphitheatre and the bas-reliefs on the tomb of Scaurus), that reproduce scenes which I have but to transfer to prose. Let us, then, suppose the twenty thousand spectators to be in their places on thirty-four ranges of seats, one above the other, around the arena; then, let us take our seats among them and look on.

First we have a hunt. A panther, secured by a long rope to the neck of a bull let loose, is set on against a young *bestiarius*, who holds two javelins in his hands. A man, armed with a long lance, irritates the bull so that it may move and second the rush of the panther fastened to it. The lad who has the javelins, and is a novice in his business, is but making his first attempt; should the bull not move, he runs no risk, yet I should not like to be in his place.

Then follows a more serious combat between a bear and a man, who irritates him by holding out a cloth at him, as the matadors do in bull-fights. Another group shows us a tiger and a lion escaping in different directions. An unarmed and naked man is in pursuit of the tiger, who cannot be a very cross one. But here is a *venatio* much more dramatic in its character. The nude bestiarius has just pierced a wolf through and through, and the animal is in flight with the spear sticking in his body, but the man staggers and a wild boar is rushing at him. At the same time, a stag thrown down by a lasso that is still seen dangling to his antlers, awaits his death-blow; hounds are dashing at him, and "their fierce baying echoes from vale to vale."

But that is not all. Look at yon group of victors: a real matador has plunged his spear into the breast of a bull with so violent a stroke that the point of the weapon comes out at the animal's back; and another has just brought down and impaled a bear; a dog is leaping at the throat of a fugitive wild boar and biting him; and, in this ferocious menagerie, peopled with lions and panthers, two rabbits are scampering about, undoubtedly to the great amusement of the throng. The Romans were fond of these contrasts, which furnished Galienus an opportunity to be jocosely generous. "A lapidary," says M. Magnin, "had sold the emperor's wife some jewels, which were recognized to be false; the emperor had the dishonest dealer arrested and condemned to the lions;

but when the fatal moment came, he turned no more formidable creature loose upon him than a capon. Everybody was astonished, and while all were vainly striving to guess the meaning of such an enigma, he caused the *curion*, or herald, to proclaim aloud: "This man tried to cheat, and now he is caught in his turn."

I have described the hunts at Pompeii; they were small affairs compared with those of Rome. The reader may know that Titus, who finished the Coliseum, caused five thousand animals to be killed there in a single day in the presence of eighty thousand spectators. Let us confess, however, that with this exhibition of tigers, panthers, lions, and wild boars, the provincial hunts were still quite dramatic.

I now come to the gladiatorial combats. To commence with the preliminaries of the fight, a ring-master, with his long staff in his hand, traces the circle, within which the antagonists must keep. One of the latter, half-armed, blows his trumpet and two boys behind him hold his helmet and his shield. The other has nothing, as yet, but his shield in his hand; two slaves are bringing him his helmet and his sword. The trumpet has sounded, and the ring-master and

slaves have disappeared. The gladiators are at it. One
of them has met with a mishap. The point of his sword
is bent and he has just thrown away his shield. The
blood is flowing from his arm, which he extends toward the spectators, at the same time raising his
thumb. That was the sign the vanquished made when
they asked for quarter. But the people do not grant it
this time, for they have turned the twenty thousand
thumbs of their right hands downwards. The man
must die, and the victor is advancing upon him to
slaughter him.

Would you like to see an equestrian combat? Two
horsemen are charging on each other. They wear
helmets with visors, and carry spears and the round
shield (*parma*), but they are lightly armed. Only one of
their arms—that which sustains the spear—is covered
with bands or armlets of metal. Their names and the
number of their victories already won are known.
The first is Bebrix, a barbarian, who has been triumphant fifteen times; the second is Nobilior, a Roman,
who has vanquished eleven times. The combat is still
undecided. Nobilior is just delivering a spear thrust,
which is vigorously parried by Bebrix.

Would you prefer a still more singular kind of duel — one between a *secutor* and a *retiarius?* The retiarius wears neither helmet nor cuirass, but carries a three-pronged javelin, called a trident, in his left hand, and in his right a net, which he endeavors to throw over the head of his adversary. If he misses his aim he is lost; the secutor then pursues him, sword in hand, and kills him. But in the duel at which we are present, the secutor is vanquished, and has fallen on one knee; the retiarius, Nepimus, triumphant already on five preceding occasions, has seized him by the belt, and has planted one foot upon his leg, but the trident not being sufficient to finish him, a second secutor, Hippolytus by name, who has survived five previous victories, has come up. Hippolytus rests one hand upon the helmet of the vanquished secutor who vainly clasps his knees, and with the other, cuts his throat.

Death — always death! In the paintings; in the bas-reliefs that I describe; in the scenes that they reproduce; in the arena where these combats must have taken place, I can see only unhappy wretches undergoing assassination. One of them, holding his

20

shield behind him, is thinking only how he may man-
age to fall with grace; another, kneeling, presses his
wound with one hand, and stretches the other out toward the spectators; some of them have a suppliant
look, others are stoical, but all will have to roll at last
upon the sand of the arena, condemned by the inex-
orable caprice of a people greedy for blood. "The
modest virgin," says Juvenal, "turning down her
thumb, orders that the breast of yonder man, grovel-
ling in the dust, shall be torn open." And all — the
heavily armed Samnite, the Gaul, the Thracian, the
secutor; the *dimachoerus*, with his two swords; the
swordsman who wears a helmet surmounted with a
fish — the one whom the retiarius pursues with his net,
meanwhile singing this refrain, "It is not you
that I am after, but your fish, and why do you flee
from me?" — all, all must succumb, at last, sooner or
later, were it to be after the hundredth victory, in this
same arena, where once an attendant employed in the
theatre used to come, in the costume of Mercury, to
touch them with a red-hot iron to make sure that they
were dead. If they moved, they were at once dis-
patched; if they remained icy-cold and motionless, a

slave harpooned them with a hook, and dragged them through the mire of sand and blood to the narrow corridor, the *porta libitinensis*, — the portal of death, — whence they were flung into the spoliarium, so that their arms and clothing, at least, might be saved. Such were the games of the amphitheatre.

IX.

THE ERUPTION.

It was during one of these festivals, on the 23d of November, 79, that the terrible eruption which overwhelmed the city burst forth. The testimony of the ancients, the ruins of Pompeii, the layers upon layers of ashes and scoriæ that covered it, the skeletons surprised in attitudes of agony or death, all concur to tell us of the catastrophe. The imagination can add nothing to it: the picture is there before our eyes; we are present at the scene; we behold it. Seated in the amphitheatre, we take to flight at the first convulsions, at the first lurid flashes which announce the conflagration and the crumbling of the mountain. The ground is shaken repeatedly; and something like a whirlwind

(232)

of dust, that grows thicker and thicker, has gone rushing and spinning across the heavens. For some days past there has been talk of gigantic forms, which, sometimes on the mountain and sometimes in the plain, swept through the air; they are up again now, and rear themselves to their whole height in the eddies of smoke, from amid which is heard a strange sound, a fearful moaning followed by claps of thunder that crash down, peal on peal. Night, too, has come on — a night of horror; enormous flames kindle the darkness like the blaze of a furnace. People scream, out in the streets, " Vesuvius is on fire!"

On the instant, the Pompeians, terrified, bewildered, rush from the amphitheatre, happy in finding so many places of exit through which they can pour forth without crushing each other, and the open gates of the city only a short distance beyond. However, after the first explosion, after the deluge of ashes, comes the deluge of fire, or light stones, all ablaze, driven by the wind — one might call it a burning snow — descending slowly, inexorably, fatally, without cessation or intermission, with pitiless persistence. This solid flame blocks up the streets, piles itself in

20*

heaps on the roofs and breaks through into the houses with the crashing tiles and the blazing rafters. The fire thus tumbles in from story to story, upon the pavement of the courts, where, accumulating like earth thrown in to fill a trench, it receives fresh fuel from the red and fiery flakes that slowly, fatally, keep showering down, falling, falling, without respite.

The inhabitants flee in every direction; the strong, the youthful, those who care only for their lives, escape. The amphitheatre is emptied in the twinkling of an eye and none remain in it but the dead gladiators. But woe to those who have sought shelter in the shops, under the arcades of the theatre, or in underground retreats. The ashes surround and stifle them! Woe, above all, to those whom avarice or cupidity hold back; to the wife of Proculus, to the favorite of Sallust, to the daughters of the house of the Poet who have tarried to gather up their jewels! They will fall suffocated among these trinkets, which, scattered around them, will reveal their vanity and the last trivial cares that then beset them, to after ages. A woman in the atrium attached to the house of the Faun ran wildly as chance directed, laden with jewelry; unable any longer to get breath, she had sought refuge in the tablinum, and there strove in vain to hold up, with her outstretched arms, the ceiling crumbling in upon her. She was crushed to death, and her head was missing when they found her.

In the Street of the Tombs, a dense crowd must have jostled each other, some rushing in from the country to seek safety in the city, and others flying from the burning houses in quest of deliverance under the open sky. One of them fell foward with his feet turned toward the Herculaneum gate; another on his back, with his arms uplifted. He bore in his hands one hundred and twenty-seven silver coins and sixty-nine pieces of gold. A third victim was also on his back; and, singular fact, they all died looking toward Vesuvius!

A female holding a child in her arms had taken shelter in a tomb which the volcano shut tight upon her; a soldier, faithful to duty, had remained erect at his post before the Herculaneum gate, one hand upon his mouth and the other on his spear. In this brave attitude he perished. The family of Diomed had assembled in his cellar, where seventeen victims, women, children, and the young girl whose throat was found moulded in the ashes, were buried alive, clinging closely to each other, destroyed there by suffocation, or, perhaps, by hunger. Arrius Diomed had tried to escape alone, abandoning his house and taking with him only one slave, who carried his money-wallet. He fell, struck down by the stifling gases, in front of his own garden. How many other poor wretches there were whose last agonies have been disclosed to us!— the priest of Isis, who, enveloped in flames and unable to escape into the blazing street, cut through two walls with his axe and yielded his last breath at the foot of the third, where he had fallen with fatigue or struck down by the deluge of ashes, but still clutching his weapon. And the poor dumb brutes, tied so that they could not break away,—the mule in the bakery, the horses in the tavern of Albinus, the goat of Siricus, which had crouched into the kitchen oven, where it was recently found, with its bell still attached to its neck! And the prisoners in the blackhole of the gladiators' barracks, riveted to an iron rack that jammed their legs! And the two lovers surprised in a shop near the Thermæ; both were young, and they were tightly clasped in each other's arms. . . . . How awful a night and how fearful a morrow! Day has come, but the darkness remains; not that of a moonless night, but that of a closed room without lamp or candle. At Misenum, where Pliny the younger, who has described the catastrophe, was stationed, nothing was heard but the voices of children, of men, and of women, calling to each other, seeking each other, recognizing each other by their cries alone, invoking death, bursting out in wails and screams of anguish, and believing that it was the eternal night in which gods and men alike were rushing headlong to annihilation. Then there fell a shower of ashes so dense that, at the distance of seven leagues from the volcano, one had to shake one's clothing continually, so as not to be suffocated. These ashes went, it is said, as far as Africa, or, at all events, to Rome, where they filled the atmosphere and hid the light of day, so that even the Romans said: "The world is overturned; the sun is falling on the earth to bury itself in night, or the earth is rushing up to the sun to be consumed in his eternal fires." "At length," writes Pliny, "the light returned gradually, and the star that sheds it reappeared, but pallid as in an

eclipse. The whole scene around us was transformed; the ashes, like a heavy snow, covered everything. "

This vast shroud was not lifted until in the last century, and the excavations have narrated the catastrophe
with an eloquence which even Pliny himself, notwithstanding the resources of his style and the authority
of his testimony, could not attain. The terrible exter-
minator was caught, as it were, in the very act, amid
the ruins he had made. These roofless houses, with
the height of one story only remaining and leaving
their walls open to the sun; these colonnades that no
longer supported anything; these temples yawning
wide on all sides, without pediment or portico; this
silent loneliness; this look of desolation, distress, and
nakedness, which looked like ruins on the morrow of
some great fire,— all were enough to wring one's heart.
But there was still more: there were the skeletons
found at every step in this voyage of discovery in the
midst of the dead, betraying the anguish and the terror of that last dreadful hour. Six hundred,— perhaps
more,— have already been found, each one illustrating

Bodies of Pompeians cast in the Ashes.

some poignant episode of the immense catastrophe in which they were smitten down!

Recently, in a small street, under heaps of rubbish. the men working on the excavations perceived an empty space, at the bottom of which were some bones. They at once called Signor Fiorelli, who had a bright idea. He caused some plaster to be mixed, and poured it immediately into the hollow, and the same operation was renewed at other points where he thought he saw other similar bones. Afterward, the crust of pumice-stone and hardened ashes which had enveloped, as it were, in a scabbard, this something that they were trying to discover, was carefully lifted off. When these materials had been removed, there appeared four dead bodies.

Any one can see them now, in the museum at Naples; nothing could be more striking than the spectacle. They are not statues, but corpses, moulded by Vesuvius; the skeletons are still there, in those casings of plaster which reproduce what time would have destroyed, and what the damp ashes have preserved, — the clothing and the flesh, I might almost say the life. The bones peep through here and there, in certain places which the plaster did not reach. Nowhere else is there anything like this to be seen. The Egyptian mummies are naked, blackened, hideous; they no longer have anything in common with us; they are laid out for their eternal sleep in the consecrated attitude. But the exhumed Pompeians are human beings whom one sees in the agonies of death.

One of these bodies is that of a woman near whom were picked up ninety-one pieces of coin, two silver urns, and some keys and jewels. She was endeavoring to escape, taking with her these precious articles, when she fell down in the narrow street. You still see her lying on her left side; her head-dress can very readily be made out, as also can the texture of her clothing and two silver rings which she still has on her finger; one of her hands is broken, and you see the cellular structure of the bone; her left arm is lifted and distorted; her delicate hand is so tightly clenched that you would say the nails penetrate the flesh; her whole body appears swollen and contracted; the legs only, which are very slender, remain extended. One feels that she struggled a long time in horrible agony; her whole attitude is that of anguish, **not** of death.

Behind her had fallen a woman and a young girl; the elder of the two, the mother, perhaps, was of humble birth, to judge by the size of her ears; on her finger she had only an iron ring; her left leg lifted and contorted, shows that she, too, suffered; not so much, however, as the noble lady: the poor have less to lose in dying. Near her, as though upon the same bed, lies the young girl; one at the head, and the other at the foot, and their legs are crossed. This young girl, almost a child, produces a strange impression; one sees exactly the tissue, the stitches of her clothing, the sleeves that covered her arms almost to the wrists, some rents here and there that show the naked flesh, and the embroidery of the little shoes in which she walked; but above all, you witness her last hour, as though you had been there, beneath the wrath of Vesuvius; she had thrown her dress over her head, like the daughter of Diomed, because she was afraid; she had fallen in running, with her face to the ground, and not being able to rise again, had rested her young, frail head upon one of her arms. One of her hands was half open, as though she had been holding something, the veil, perhaps, that covered her.

21

You see the bones of her fingers penetrating the plaster. Her cranium is shining and smooth, her legs are
raised backward and placed one upon the other; she
did not suffer very long, poor child! but it is her corpse
that causes one the sorest pang to see, for she was not
more than fifteen years of age.

The fourth body is that of a man, a sort of colossus.
He lay upon his back so as to die bravely; his arms
and his limbs are straight and rigid. His clothing is
very clearly defined, the greaves visible and fitting
closely; his sandals laced at the feet, and one of them
pierced by the toe, the nails in the soles distinct; the
stomach naked and swollen like those of the other
bodies, perhaps by the effect of the water, which has
kneaded the ashes. He wears an iron ring on the
bone of one finger; his mouth is open, and some of
his teeth are missing; his nose and his cheeks stand
out prominently; his eyes and his hair have disappeared,
but the moustache still clings. There is something
martial and resolute about this fine corpse. After
the women who did not want to die, we see this man,
fearless in the midst of the ruins that are crushing
him — *impavidum ferient ruinæ.*

I stop here, for Pompeii itself can offer nothing that approaches this palpitating drama. It is violent death, with all its supreme tortures, — death that suffers and struggles, — taken in the very act, after the lapse of eighteen centuries.

ITINERARY.

AN ITINERARY.

In order to render my work less lengthy and less confused, as well as easier to read, I have grouped together the curiosities of Pompeii, according to their importance and their purport, in different chapters. I shall now mark out an itinerary, wherein they will be classed in the order in which they present themselves to the traveller, and I shall place after each street and each edifice the indication of the chapter in which I have described or named it in my work.

In approaching Pompeii by the usual entrance, which is the nearest to the railroad, it would be well to go directly to the Forum. See chap. II.

The monuments of the Forum are as follows. I have *italicized* the most curious :

The Basilica.   See chap. II.
The Temple of Venus.   "
The Curia, or Council Hall.   "
The Edifice of Eumachia.   "
The Temple of Mercury.   "
The Temple of Jupiter.
The Senate Chamber.
The Pantheon.   "

From the Forum, you will go toward the north, passing by the Arch of Triumph; visit the *Temple of Fortune* (see chap. VI.), and stop at the Thermæ (see chap. V.).

On leaving the Thermæ, pass through the entire north-west of the city, that is to say, the space comprised between the streets of Fortune and of the Thermæ and the walls. In this space are comprised the following edifices:

247

The House of Pansa. See chap. VI.

The House of the Tragic Poet. Chap. **VII.**

The Fullonica. Chap. III.

The Mosaic Fountains. Chap. VII.

The House of Adonis. Chap. VII.

The House of Apollo.

The House of Meleager.

The House of the Centaur.

The House of Castor and Pollux. Chap. **VII.**

The House of the Anchor.

The House of Polybius.

The House of the Academy of Music.

The Bakery. See chap. III.

The House of Sallust. Chap. VII.

The Public Oven.

A Fountain. Chap. III.

The House of the Dancing Girls.

The Perfumery Shop. Chap III.

The House of Three Stories.

The Custom House. Chap. IV.

The House of the Surgeon. Chap. **III.**

The House of the Vestal Virgins.

The Shop of Albinus.

The Thermopolium. Chap. III.

Thus you arrive at the *Walls* and at the Gate of Herculaneum, beyond which the *Street of the Tombs* opens and the suburbs develop. All this is described in chap. IV.

Here are the monuments in the Street of the Tombs:

The Sentry Box.   See Chap. IV.

The Tomb of Mamia.   "

The Tomb of Ferentius.   "

The Sculptor's Atelier.

The Tomb with the Wreaths.

The Public Bank.

The House of the Mosaic Columns.

The Villa of Cicero.

The Tomb of Scaurus.

The Round Tomb.   See Chap. **iv.**
The Tomb with the Marble Door.   "
The Tomb of Libella.   "
The Tomb of Calventius.
The Tomb of Nevoleia Tyché.
The Funereal Triclinium.
The Tomb of Labeo.
The Tombs of the Arria Family.
The Villa of Diomed.

Having visited these tombs, re-enter the city by the **Herculaneum Gate**, and, returning over part of the way already taken, **find the** Street of Fortune again, and there see —

The House of the Faun.   Chap. **vii.**
The House with the Black Wall.
The House with the Figured Capitals.
The House of the Grand Duke.
The House of Ariadne.
The House of the Hunt.   Chap. **vii.**

You thus reach the place where the Street of Stabiæ turns to the right, descending toward the southern part of the city. Before taking this street, you will do well to follow the one in which you already are to where it ends at the *Nola Gate*, which is worth seeing. See chap. **iv.**

The Street of Stabiæ marks the limit reached by the excavations. To the left, in going down, you will find the handsome *House of Lucretius*. See chap. **vii.**

On the right begins a whole quarter recently discovered and not yet marked out on the diagram. Get them to show you —

The House of Siricus.   Chap. **vii.**
The Hanging Balconies.   Chap. **iii.**
The New Bakery.   Chap. **iii.**

Turning to the left, below the the Street of Stabiæ you will cross the open fields, above the part of the city not yet cleared, as far as the *Amphitheatre*. See chap. **viii.**

Then, retracing your steps and intersecting the Street of Stabiæ, you enter a succession of streets, comparatively wide, which will lead you back to the Forum. You will there find, on your right, the *Hot Baths of Stabiæ*.   See chap. v.   On your left is the *House of Cornelius Rufus* and that of *Proculus*, recently discovered.   See chap. VII.

There now remains for you to cross the *Street of Abundance* at the southern extremity of the city.   It is the quarter of the triangular Forum, and of the Theatres — the most interesting of all.

The principal monuments to be seen are —

The Temple of Isis.   See chap. VII.

The Curia Isiaca.

The Temple of Hercules.   Chap. VII.

The Grand Theatre.   Chap. VIII.

The Smaller Theatre.   "

The Barracks of the Gladiators.   Chap. VIII.

At the farther end of these barracks opens a small gate by which you may leave the city, after having made the tour of it in three hours, on this first excursion.   On your second visit you will be able to go about without a guide.

Charles Scribner & Co.,

654 Broadway, New York,

HAVE JUST COMMENCED THE PUBLICATION OF

The Illustrated Library of Wonders.

———————◆———————

This Library is based upon a similar series of works now in course of issue in France, the popularity of which may be inferred from the fact that

OVER ONE MILLION COPIES

have been sold. The volumes to be comprised in the series are all written in a popular style, and, where scientific subjects are treated of, with careful accuracy, and with the purpose of embodying the latest discoveries and inventions, and the results of the most recent developments in every department of investigation. Familiar explanations are given of the most striking phenomena in nature, and of the various operations and processes in science and the arts. Occasionally notable passages in history and remarkable adventures are described. The different volumes are profusely illustrated with engravings, designed by the most skilful artists, and executed in the most careful manner, and every possible care will be taken to render them complete and reliable expositions of the subjects upon which they respectively treat. For THE FAMILY LIBRARY, for use as PRIZES in SCHOOLS, as an inexhaustible fund of ANECDOTE and ILLUSTRATION for TEACHERS, and as works of instruction and amusement for readers of all ages, the volumes comprising THE ILLUS TRATED LIBRARY OF WONDERS will be found unexcelled.

The following volumes of the series have been published :—

Optical Wonders.

THE WONDERS OF OPTICS.—By F. Marion. Illustrated with over seventy engravings on wood, many of them full-page, and a colored frontispiece. One volume, 12mo. Price $1 50

For specimen illustration see page 81.

In the *Wonders of Optics*, the phenomena of Vision, including the structure of the eye, optical illusions, the illusions caused by light itself, and the influence of the imagination, are explained. These explanations are not at all abstract or scientific. Numerous striking facts and events, many of which were once attributed to supernatural causes, are narrated, and from them the laws in accordance with which they were developed are derived. The closing section of the book is devoted to Natural Magic, and the properties of Mirrors, the Stereoscope, the Spectroscope, &c., &c., are fully described, together with the methods by which "Chinese Shadows," Spectres, and numerous other illusions are produced. The book is one which furnishes an almost illimitable fund of amusement and instruction, and it is illustrated with no less than 73 finely executed engravings, many of them full-page.

CRITICAL NOTICES.

"The work has the merit of conveying much useful scientific information in a popular manner."—*Phila. North American.*

"Thoroughly admirable, and as an introduction to this science for the general reader, leaves hardly anything to be desired."—*N. Y. Evening Post.*

"Treats in a charming, but scientific and exhaustive manner, the wonderful subject of optics."—*Cleveland Leader.*

" All the marvels of light and of optical illusions are made clear."—*N. Y. Observer.*

Thunder and Lightning.

THUNDER AND LIGHTNING. By W. De Fonvielle. Illustrated with 39 Engravings on wood, nearly all full-page. One volume. 12mo $1 50

For specimen illustrations see page 14.

Thunder and Lightning, as its title indicates, deals with the most startling phenomena of nature. The writings of the author, M. De Fonvielle, have attracted very general attention in France, as well on account of the happy manner in which he calls his readers' attention to certain facts heretofore treated in scientific works only, as because of the statement of others often observed and spoken of, over which he appears to throw quite a new light. The different kinds of lightning—forked, globular, and sheet lightning—are described; numerous instances of the effects produced by this wonderful agency are very graphically narrated; and thirty-nine engravings, nearly all full-page, illustrate the text most effectively. The volume is certain to excite popular interest, and to call the attention of persons unaccustomed to observe to some of the wonderful phenomena which surround us in this world.

CRITICAL NOTICES.

"In the book before us the dryness of detail is avoided. The author has given us all the scientific information necessary, and yet so happily united interest with instruction that no person who has the smallest particle of curiosity to investigate the subject treated of can fail to be interested in it."—*N. Y. Herald.*

"Any boy or girl who wants to read strange stories and see curious pictures of the doings of electricity, had better get these books."—*Our Young Folks.*

"A volume which cannot fail to attract attention and awaken interest in persons who have not been accustomed to give the subject any thought."—*Daily Register (New Haven).*

ℌeat.

THE WONDERS OF HEAT. By ACHILLE CAZIN. With 90 illustrations, many of them full-page, and a colored frontispiece. One volume, 12mo $1 50

For specimen illustration see page 15.

In the *Wonders of Heat* the principal phenomena are presented as viewed from the standpoint afforded by recent discoveries. Burning-glasses, and the remarkable effects produced by them, are described; the relations between heat and electricity, between heat and cold, and the comparative effects of each, are discussed; and incidentally, interesting accounts are given of the mode of formation of glaciers, of Montgolfier's balloon, of Davy's safety-lamp, of the methods of glass-blowing, and of numerous other facts in nature and processes in art dependent upon the influence of heat. Like the other volumes of the Library of Wonders, this is illustrated wherever the text gives an opportunity for explanation by this method.

CRITICAL NOTICES.

"From the first to the very last page the interest is all-absorbing."—*Albany Evening Times.*

"The book deserves, as it will doubtless attain. a wide circulation."—*Pittsburg Chron*

"This book is instructive and clear."—*Independent.*

"It describes and explains the wonders of heat in a manner to be clearly understood by non-scientific readers."—*Phila. Inquirer.*

Animal Intelligence.

THE INTELLIGENCE OF ANIMALS, WITH ILLUSTRATIVE ANECDOTES.—From the French of ERNEST MENAULT. With 54 illustrations. One volume, 12mo . $1 50

For specimen illustration see page 16.

In this very interesting volume there are grouped together a great number of facts and anecdotes collected from original sources, and from the writings of the most eminent naturalists of all countries, designed to illustrate the manifestations of intelligence in the animal creation. Very many novel and curious facts regarding the habits of Reptiles, Birds, and Beasts are narrated in the most charming style, and in a way which is sure to excite the desire of every reader for wider knowledge of one of the most fascinating subjects in the whole range of natural history. The grace and skill displayed in the illustrations, which are very numerous, make the volume singularly attractive.

CRITICAL NOTICES.

"May be recommended as very entertaining."—*London Athenæum.*

"The stories are of real value to those who take any interest in the curious habits of animals."—*Rochester Democrat.*

Egypt.

EGYPT 3,300 YEARS AGO; OR, RAMESES THE GREAT. By F. DE LANOYE. With 40 illustrations. One volume, 12mo $1 50

For specimen illustration see page 17.

This volume is devoted to the wonders of Ancient Egypt during the time of the Pharaohs and under Sesostris, the period of its greatest splendor and magnificence. Her monuments, her palaces, her pyramids, and her works of art are not only accurately described in the text, but reproduced in a series of very attractive illustrations as they have been restored by French explorers, aided by students of Egyptology. While the volume has the attraction of being devoted to a subject which possesses all the charms of novelty to the great number of readers, it has the substantial merit of discussing, with intelligence and careful accuracy, one of the greatest epochs in the world's history.

CRITICAL NOTICES.

"I think this a good book for the purpose for which it is designed. It is brief on each head, lively and graphic, without any theatrical artifices; is not the work of a novice, but of a real scholar in Egyptology, and, as far as can be ascertained now, is history."— *JAMES C. MOFFAT, Professor in Princeton Theological Seminary.*

"The volume is full of wonders."—*Hartford Courant.*

"Evidently prepared with great care."—*Chicago Evening Journal.*

"Not merely the curious in antiquarian matters will find this volume attractive, but the general reader will be pleased, entertained, and informed by it."—*Portland Argus.*

"The work possesses the freshness and charm of romance, and cannot fail to repay all who glance over its pages."—*Philadelphia City Item.*

Great Hunts.

ADVENTURES ON THE GREAT HUNTING GROUNDS OF THE WORLD. By VICTOR MEUNIER. Illustrated with 22 woodcuts.   One volume 12mo .   . $1 50

For specimen illustration see page 18.

Besides numerous thrilling adventures judiciously selected, this work contains much valuable and exceedingly interesting information regarding the different animals, adventures with which are narrated, together with accurate descriptions of the different countries, making the volume not only interesting, but instructive in a remarkable degree.

CRITICAL NOTICES.

"This is a very attractive volume in this excellent series."—*Cleveland Herald.*

"Cannot fail to prove entertaining to the juvenile reader."—*Albion.*

"The adventures are gathered from the histories of famous travellers and explorers, and have the merit of truth as well as interest."—*N. Y. Observer.*

"Just the book for boys during the coming Winter evenings."—*Boston Daily Journal.*

Pompeii.

WONDERS OF POMPEII.   By MARC MONNIER. With 22 illustrations.   One volume 12mo .   . $1 50

For specimen illustration see page 19.

There are here summed up, in a very lively and graphic style, the results of the discoveries made at Pompeii since the commencement of the extensive excavations there.   The illustrations represent the houses, the domestic utensils, the statues, and the various works of art, as investigation gives every reason to believe that they existed at the time of the eruption.

Sublime in Nature.

THE SUBLIME IN NATURE, FROM DESCRIP-
TIONS OF CELEBRATED TRAVELLERS AND
WRITERS. By FERDINAND LANOYE. Illustrated with 48 wood-
cuts.   One volume 12mo $1 50

For specimen illustration see page 20.

The Air and Atmospheric Phenomena, the Ocean, Mountains, Volcanic
Phenomena, Rivers, Falls and Cataracts, Grottoes and Caverns, and the
Phenomena of Vegetation, are described in this volume, and in the most
charming manner possible, because the descriptions given have been selected
from the writings of the most distinguished authors and travellers. The
illustrations, several of which are from the pencil of GUSTAVE DORÉ, reproduce scenes in this country, as well as in foreign lands.

The Sun.

THE SUN. By AMEDEE GUILLEMIN.   From the French
by T. L. PHIPSON, Ph.D.   With 58 illustrations.   One
volume 12mo $1 50

For specimen illustration see page 21.

M. GUILLEMIN'S well-known work upon *The Heavens* has secured him
a wide reputation as one of the first of living astronomical writers and observers. In this compact treatise he discourses familiarly but most accurately and entertainingly of the Sun as the source of light, of heat, and of
chemical action; of its influence upon living beings; of its place in the
Planetary World; of its place in the Sidereal World; of its physical and

chemical constitution ; of the maintenance of Solar Radiation, and, in conclusion, the question whether the Sun is inhabited, is examined. The work
embraces the results of the most recent investigations, and is valuable for
its fulness and accuracy as well as for the very popular way in which the
subject is presented.

CRITICAL NOTICES.

"The matter of the volume is highly interesting, as well as scientifically complete ; the
style is clear and simple, and the illustrations excellent."—*N. Y. Daily Tribune.*

" For the first time, the fullest and latest information about the Sun has been comprised
in a single volume."—*Philadelphia Press.*

"The work is intensely interesting. It is written in a style which must commend itself
to the general reader, and imparts a vast fund of information in language free from astrono
mical or other scientific technicalities."—*Albany Evening Journal.*

"The latest discoveries of science are set forth in a popular and attractive style."—*Portland Transcript.*

" Conveys, in a graphic form, the present amount of knowledge in regard to the luminous
centre of our solar system."—*Boston Congregationalist.*

Glass=Making.

WONDERS OF GLASS-MAKING ; Its Description
and History from the Earliest Times to the
Present. By A. Sauzay. With 63 illustrations on wood. One
volume 12mo $1 50

For specimen illustration see page 22.

The title of this work very accurately indicates its character. It is written in an exceedingly lively and graphic style, and the useful and ornamental applications of glass are fully described. The illustrations represent,
among other things, the mirror of Marie de Medici and various articles
manufactured from glass which have, from their unique character, or the
associations connected with them, acquired historical interest.

CRITICAL NOTICES.

" All the information which the general reader needs on the subject will be found here
in a very intelligible and attractive form."—*N. Y. Evening Post.*

"Tells about every branch of this curious manufacture, tracing its progress from the re-
motest ages, and omitting not one point upon which information can be desired "—*Boston
Post.*

" A very useful and interesting book."—*N. Y. Citizen.*

Italian Art.

WONDERS OF ITALIAN ART.   By LOUIS VIARDOT.
With 28 illustrations.   One volume 12mo   . $1 50

For specimen illustration see page 23.

As a compact, readable, and instructive manual upon a subject the exposition of which has heretofore been confined to ambitious and expensive treatises, this volume has no equal.   In style it is clear and attractive ; its critical estimates are based upon thorough and extensive knowledge and sound judgment, and the illustrations reproduce, as accurately as wood engravings can do, the leading works of the famous Italian masters, while anecdotes of these great artists and curious facts regarding their works give popular interest to the volume.

The Human Body.

WONDERS OF THE HUMAN BODY.   From the
French of A. LE PILEUR, Doctor of Medicine.   Illustrated by 45 Engravings by LEVEILLÉ.   One volume 12mo   . $1 50

For specimen illustration see page 24.

While sufficiently minute in anatomical and physiological details to satisfy those who desire to go deeper into such studies than many may deem necessary, this work is nevertheless written so that it may form part of the domestic library.   Mothers and daughters may read it without being repelled or shocked ; and the young will find their interest sustained by incidental digressions to more attractive matters.   Such are the pages referring to phrenology and to music, which accompany the anatomical description of the skull and of the organs of voice ; and the chapter on artistic expression which closes the book.   Numerous simple but attractive engravings elucidate the work.

Architecture.

WONDERS OF ARCHITECTURE. Translated from the French of M. LEFÉVRE ; to which is added a chaptei on English Architecture by R. DONALD. With 50 illustrations. One volume 12mo $1 50

For specimen illustration see page 25.

The object of the *Wonders of Architecture* is to supply, in as accessible and popular a form as the nature of the subject admits, a connected and comprehensive sketch of the chief architectural achievements of ancient and modern times. Commencing with the rudest dawnings of architectural science as exemplified in the Celtic monuments, a carefully compiled and authentic record is given of the most remarkable temples, palaces, columns, towers, cathedrals, bridges, viaducts, churches, and buildings of every description which the genius of man has constructed ; and as these are all described in chronological order, according to the eras to which they belong, they form a connected narrative of the development of architecture, in which the history and progress of the art can be authentically traced. Care has been taken to popularize the theme as much as possible, to make the descriptions plain and vivid, to render the text free from mere techni calities, and to convey a correct and truthful impression of the various objects that are enumerated.

Ocean Depths.

BOTTOM OF THE SEA. By L. SONREL. Translated and edited by ELIHU RICH, translator of "Cazin's Heat," &c., with 68 woodcuts. (*Printed on Tinted Paper*) One vol 12mo $1 50

For specimen illustration see page 26.

Written in a popular and attractive style, this volume affords much use- ful information about the sea, its depth, color, and temperature ; its action in deep water and on the shores ; the exuberance of life in the depths of the ocean, and the numberless phenomena, anecdotes, adventures, and perils connected therewith. The illustrations are very numerous, and specially graphic and attractive.

CRITICAL NOTICE.

This book is well illustrated throughout, and is admirably adapted to those who require light scientific reading.—*Nature.*

Lighthouses and Lightships.

LIGHTHOUSES AND LIGHTSHIPS. By W. H. D. ADAMS. With sixty illustrations. One volume 12mo. *Printed on tinted paper* $1 50

The aim of this volume is to furnish in a popular and intelligible form a description of the Lighthouse *as it is* and *as it was,* of the rude Roman pharos, or old sea-tower, with its flickering fire of wood or coal, and the modern Lighthouse, shapely and yet substantial, with its powerful illuminating apparatus of lamps and lenses, shining ten, or twelve, or twenty miles across the waters. The author gives a descriptive and historical account of their mode of construction and organization, based on the best authorities, and revised by competent critics. Sketches are furnished of the most remarkable Lighthouses in the Old World, and a graphic narration is presented of the mode of life of their keepers.

CRITICAL NOTICES.

"The book is full of interest."—*N. Y. Commercial Advertiser.*

"The whole subject is treated in a manner at once interesting and instructive."—*Rochester Democrat.*

"The illustrations are full, and excellently engraved."—*Phil. Morning Post.*

Acoustics.

THE WONDERS OF ACOUSTICS; or, THE PHENOMEMA OF SOUND. By R. RADAU. With 110 illustrations. One volume 12mo. *Printed on tinted paper* . . $1 50

For specimen illustration see page 27.

No overweight of technicalities encumber the author's ample and exceedingly instructive disquisition; but by presenting the results of curious investigation, by anecdote, by all manner of striking illustration, and by the aid of numerous pictures, he throws a popular interest about one of the most suggestive and beautiful of the sciences. The book opens with an attractive chapter on "Sound in Nature," in which the language of animals, nocturnal life in the forests, and kindred subjects are discussed. Among the topics treated of later in the work are such as "Effects of Sound, on Living Beings," "Velocity of Sound," "The Notes," "The Voice, Music, and Science." This volume forms a valuable addition to the series.

𝕭𝖔𝖉𝖎𝖑𝖞 𝕾𝖙𝖗𝖊𝖓𝖌𝖙𝖍 𝖆𝖓𝖉 𝕾𝖐𝖎𝖑𝖑.

W ONDERS OF BODILY STRENGTH AND SKILL. Translated and enlarged from the French of GUILLAUME DEPPING, by CHARLES RUSSELL. Illustrated with seventy engravings on wood, many of them full page. One vol. 12mo. *Printed on tinted paper* **$1 50**

For specimen illustration see page 28.

This is decidedly one of the most interesting volumes of the Library of Wonders. In it the author has collected, from every available source, anecdotes descriptive of the most remarkable exhibitions of Physical Strength and Skill, whether in the form of individual feats, or of national games, from the earliest ages down to the present time. The author has simply endeavored to make a collection of " Wonders of Bodily Strength and Skill," from the Literature of all countries, and if any of them may be assigned to the region of the improbable, he most respectfully refers doubting inquirers to the original sources. The grace and skill displayed in the illustrations, which are numerous and striking, make the volume singularly attractive.

𝕭𝖆𝖑𝖑𝖔𝖔𝖓𝖘.

W ONDERFUL BALLOON ASCENTS, From the French of F. MARION. With thirty illustrations on wood, many of them full page One volume 12mo. *Printed on tinted paper* **$1 50**

For specimen illustration see page 29.

This volume gives an interesting history of balloons and balloon voyages, written in an exceedingly readable and graphic style, which will commend itself to the reader.

The history of the balloon is fully narrated, from its first stages up to the present time, and the most memorable balloon voyages are herein described in a most thrilling manner. The illustrations are exceedingly taken in character.

CRITICAL NOTICE.

" Written in a popular style and with illustrations that give completeness to the text, ... beautifully illustrated, and w ll be a fascinating reading book, especially for the young."—*London Books*.*ller.*

𝔚𝔬𝔫𝔡𝔢𝔯𝔣𝔲𝔩 𝔈𝔰𝔠𝔞𝔭𝔢𝔰.

WONDERFUL ESCAPES. Revised from the French of F. BERNARD, and original chapters added by RICHARD WHITEING. With twenty-six full-page plates. One volume 12mo. *Printed on tinted paper* . . . $1 50

For specimen illustration see page 30.

This volume of the "Library of Wonders" is an exceedingly interesting addition to the series, narrating as it does in the most thrilling manner the wonderful escapes of noted prisoners, political as well as criminal. The escapes of over forty well known personages are described in this book, and their history may be relied upon as entirely accurate, obtained from official sources. Among the characters treated of we may mention Marius, Benvenuto Cellini, Grotius, Cardinal de Retz, Baron Trenck, and Marie de Medicis. A number of full-page plates picturing the prisoners in the most fearful moments of their escapes accompany the volume.

𝔗𝔥𝔢 𝔥𝔢𝔞𝔳𝔢𝔫𝔰.

WONDERS OF THE HEAVENS. By CAMILLE FLAMMARION. From the French by Mrs. NORMAN LOCKYER. With forty-eight illustrations. One volume, 12mo . . $1 50

For specimen illustration see page 32.

M. FLAMMARION is excelled by none in that peculiar tact, which is so rare, of bringing within popular comprehension the great facts of Astronomical Science. Familiar illustrations and a glowing and eloquent style, make this volume one of the most valuable, as it is one of the most comprehensive manuals extant upon the absorbingly interesting subject of which it treats.

ALSO IN PRESS:

WONDERS OF ENGRAVING,   WONDERS OF VEGETATION,
WONDERS OF SCULPTURE,   THE INVISIBLE WORLD,
ELECTRICITY,   HYDRAULICS.

Due announcement of the appearance of the above new issues of this series will be given hereafter as they approach completion.

Specimen Illustrations

FROM

The Illustrated Library of Wonders.

THUNDER AND LIGHTNING.

By W. DE FONVIELLE.

With 39 engravings, nearly all full-page.   One volume, 12mo, $1 50.

Bell-ringer struck by Lightning.

For description of book, see page 2.

THE WONDERS OF HEAT.

By ACHILLE CAZIN.

With 90 illustrations, and a colored frontispiece. One vol. 12mo $1 50

FIG. 25 a.—Bernières' Immense Burning-glass.

For description of book, see page 3.

THE INTELLIGENCE OF ANIMALS

WITH ILLUSTRATIVE ANECDOTES.

With 54 illustrations.   One volume, 12mo, $1 50.

THE DRAKE LEADING THE LADY TO THE RESCUE.

EGYPT 3,300 YEARS AGO.

By F. DE LANOYE.

With 40 illustrations. One vo'ume, 12mo, $1 50.

The Sphinx of Rameses II. (according to the Sphinx at the Louvre)

For description of book, see page 4.

ADVENTURES ON THE

GREAT HUNTING GROUNDS OF THE WORLD.

Illustrated with 22 woodcuts.   One volume, 12mo., $1 50.

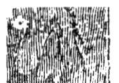

POMPEII AND THE POMPEIANS.
By MARC MONNIER.
With 30 Illustrations. One volume, 12mo, $1 50.

Discovery in a bake shop of bread baked 1800 years ago.

THE SUBLIME IN NATURE.

From Descriptions of Celebrated Writers and Travellers.

Illustrated with 38 full-page engravings.　One vol. 12mo.　Price, $1 50.

A GORGE IN THE PYRENEES.

THE SUN.

By AMEDEE GUILLEMIN.

From the French by T L. PHIPSON Ph.D   With 58 illustrations.   One vol. 12mo, $1 50.

Saturn   Uranus   Neptune   Earth

WONDERS OF GLASS-MAKING;

Its Description and History from the Earliest Times to the Present.

By A SAUZAY.

With 67 illustrations on wood.   One vol. 12mo, $1 50.

By LOUIS VIARDOT.

With 28 illustrations.   One vol. 12mo, $1 50.

DEATH OF ST. PETER MARTYR.—BY TITIAN.

Formerly in the Church of St. John and St. Pau', Venice

WONDERS OF THE HUMAN BODY.

By A. PILEUR, M.D.

With   illustrations, and a colored frontispiece.   One vol. 12mo, $1 50.

WONDERS OF ARCHITECTURE.

By ANDRE LEFEVRE.

With a Chapter on English Architecture, by R. DONALD.
One vol. 12mo, with 56 illustrations.

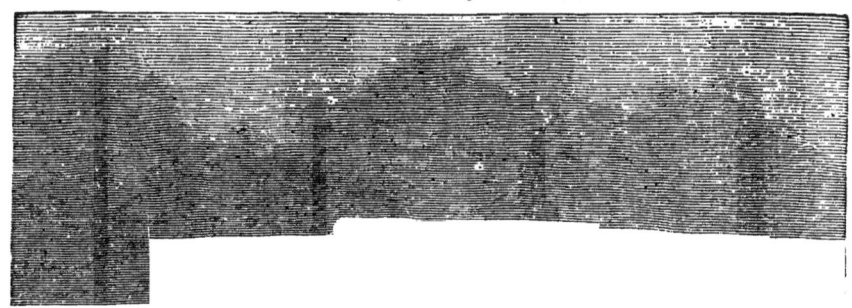

THE BOTTOM OF THE SEA.

By L. SONREL.

Translated and edited by ELIHU RICH, with 67 illustrations.   One vol. 12mo, $1 50.

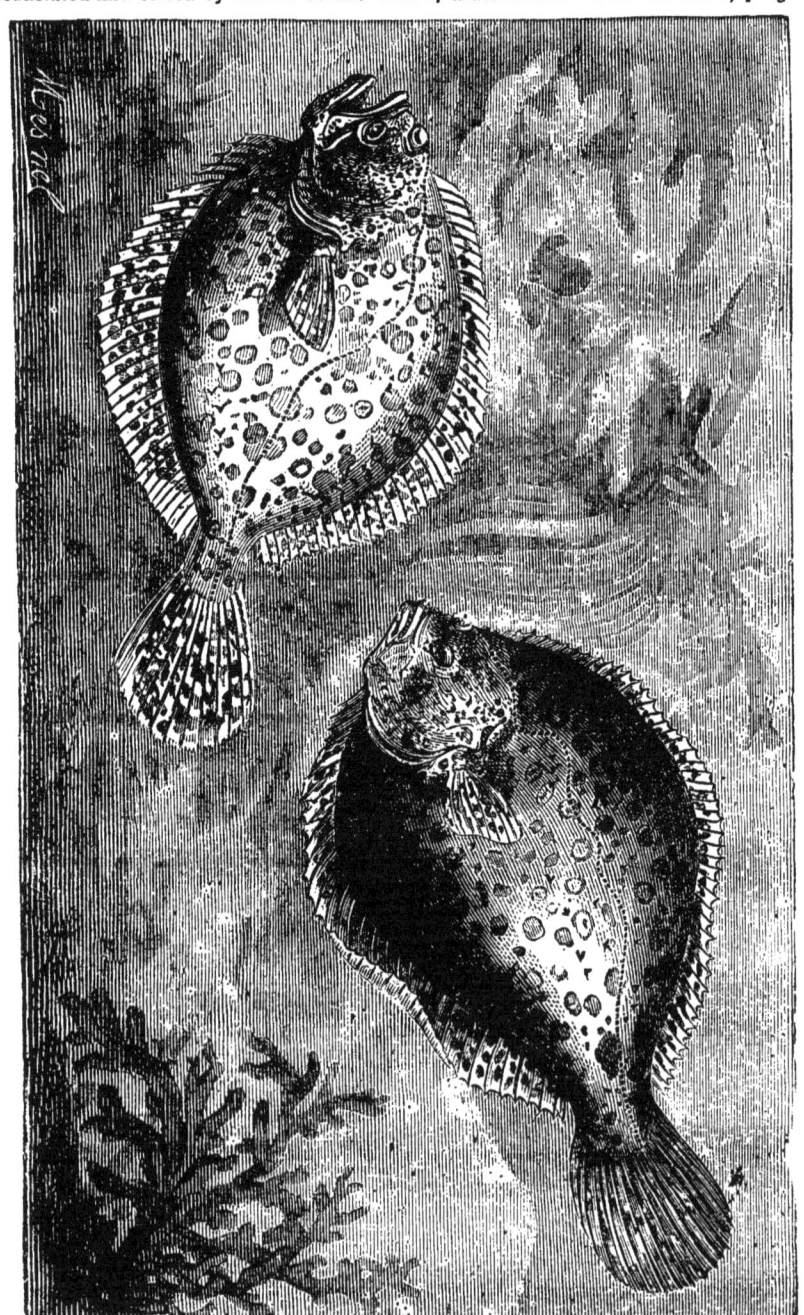

TURBOT.

THE WONDERS OF ACOUSTICS

By R. RADAU.

With 110 illustrations.   One vol. 12mo.   Price, $1 50.

THEATRE OF VITRUVIUS.

THE WONDERS OF OPTICS.

By F. MARION.

With over seventy engravings, and a colored frontispiece.   One vol. 12mo.   Price $1 50.

Fig. 55.—Wizard Dance.